D1322731

Healing Miracles

Also by Rex Gardner

Abortion: the Personal Dilemma (Paternoster Press)
What about Abortion? (Paternoster Press)
Ethical Dilemmas in Modern Contraceptive Developments (The Rendle
Short Lecture for 1973) (CMF)
By What Standard? (CMF)

Healing Miracles

A doctor investigates

REX GARDNER

Darton, Longman and Todd
London

First published in 1986 by
Darton, Longman and Todd Ltd
89 Lillie Road, London SW6 1UD

Reprinted 1987 and 1988

© 1986 Rex Gardner

ISBN 0 232 51640 5

British Library Cataloguing in Publication Data

Gardner, Rex
  Healing miracles : a doctor investigates.
  1. Spiritual healing
  I. Title
  615.8'52   BT732.5

  ISBN 0–232–51640–5

Phototypeset by
Input Typesetting Ltd, London SW19 8DR
Printed and bound in Great Britain by
Anchor Brendon Ltd, Tiptree, Essex

DEDICATED
IN GRATITUDE AND AFFECTION
TO MY FELLOW MEMBERS OF THE
CHRISTIAN MEDICAL FELLOWSHIP

Contents

Acknowledgements   ix

Introduction   1

1   Miracles: a possibility worth investigating?   10

2   Miracles: is some other explanation possible?   23

3   The Church and Healing   42

4   Miracles: a constant phenomenon?   67

5   A New Pentecost?   93

6   The Biblical Basis for Miracles   110

7   Miracles: temporary phenomena or permanent gift?   130

8   Is the Christian entitled to claim Physical Healing?   155

9   God's Strange Work   175

10   Where have we got to?   187

Index   209

Acknowledgements

In addition to those mentioned in the text, I would like to thank the following members of the medical profession who have allowed me access to medical records or have given detailed answers to my queries: Dr M. Ansdell-Smith, Dr P. Dale, Mr J. Gunn, Dr C. Hawkes, Mr A. Jefferson, Dr I. Kerr, Dr L. Le Dune, Mr R. Jameson, Miss M. L. Langdon-Stokes, Dr I. Longfield, Dr Rhiannon Lloyd, Mr R. Lunt, Dr J. Maitland, Dr A. Malcolm, Dr J. Rhodes, Dr W. Stockdale, Mr D. Thomas, the Revd S. Thomas FRCS, Dr Mary Thomson, Dr A. Townsend, Professor J. Webb. As some of these colleagues would not wish to be associated with the conclusions I draw, I am particularly appreciative of their helpfulness.

A great number of other people have helped me in various ways. To name them all would be impracticable. The following have helped with details of case histories: Mr and Mrs Beaumont, Miss D. Collingham, Dr and Mrs R. Dennis, Mrs E. D'Souza, Sister Ruth and Sister Eulalia of the Evangelical Sisters of Mary, Mr R. Hawes, Mr E. Jefferies of the Pin Mill Christian Healing Centre, Mrs J. McGurk, Mrs D. Murtha, Pastor F. Smith, Mr J. Sture, and the Revd M. Turner. I am also grateful to other friends who have pointed me towards case histories, some of which I hope to explore in the future.

I have observed medical ethical practice in withholding the names of doctors and patients in the cases described, but made an exception in some cases which have already been published and the persons already named. Permission has been given, by the patients concerned, and by the doctors whose help I have sought, for me to use these cases.

Acknowledgements

Technical details have been provided where it seems necessary as medical evidence; it would be unwise for the lay reader to attempt to construe anything from them.

I am grateful to my son Dr Iain Gardner, a patristic scholar, for giving me St Augustine's *City of God* and for insisting that I study Martin of Tours; and to Dr Clare Stancliffe who answered my questions on Martin.

I am grateful to the Editor of the *British Medical Journal* for permission to develop material from my article which appeared in 1983; to the Editor of *Christian Medical Fellowship* for permission to quote from R. Jameson's article in *In the Service of Medicine* (1984); and to the Editor of *Today* for the quotation from 'Miracles; the Mystery and the Meaning' by John Pridmore, published in *Crusade* (1976).

Particular thanks are due to the many Christian friends, medical and otherwise, who have shared with me their experience of God's healing work today; and to members of the local church house-group who have supported me by their prayers, and to one of its leaders – Ailsa Granne – who has critically read the manuscript.

I must make it crystal clear that the views expressed are solely my own, and not necessarily shared by any other person or organisation mentioned in the work.

It is customary to thank one's wife and family on such occasions. In this case that is no formality. There have been considerable periods when, in addition to her busy professional work as an ophthalmologist, my wife has had to run the home as a 'one parent family', in order to let me get on with this writing. One of my sons has had to put up with his room doubling as my word-processing studio. Another has had to teach me how to use it and, while away at university, come to the telephone to answer my cries for help!

Lastly, I would like to record my gratitude to Lesley Riddle of Darton, Longman and Todd for her invitation to write this book, and for her patience while awaiting the manuscript.

REX GARDNER

Introduction

When I was going through a patient's NHS notes recently, some words in the green ink I favoured ten years ago stood out: 'Part of this woman's problem is her conviction that as a Christian she should not be ill. Therefore she is in a cleft stick; either God is letting her down, or she is letting God down.'

Those sentences formed part of my referral note of this patient to a psychiatric colleague. That course of action displays the practical dilemma faced by Christians in the clinical situation. There is no shortage of writing on 'divine healing': there appears to me to be an acute shortage of writing addressing itself to the practical and clamant problems not only of the Christian who is ill, but of the doctor or the Christian counsellor. This book is written for those people at the sharp end who need to know with some urgency where they and their patients stand as regards miraculous healing.

In Uganda my ward round was interrupted one day by the arrival of an expatriate family who had been involved in a road accident: the small son was dead; grandmother had horrendous bilateral hip injuries. They had been sustained while swerving to avoid a cow on the road. In my present journey there is a whole herd of sacred cows on the road. I do not intend to swerve to avoid any of them.

Let me be clear what we are discussing in this work. By miraculous healing I mean the healing of organic disease by means, or at a speed, inexplicable medically and preceded by prayer in the name of Jesus Christ.

Miracles have exercised some of the most able minds. Ian

1

Ramsey, for his inaugural lecture in the Chair of Christian Philosophy at Oxford, took the topic, 'Miracles: an exercise in logical mapwork',[1] a stimulating read provided there is an ample supply of black coffee. Many other philosophers and theologians have dealt with the issue but few of their books tackle the urgent questions of the patient whose doctor utters the dreadful word 'cancer'; or the dilemma of the Christian doctor who, having reached the end of the therapeutic road, is asked if prayer might work; or the medical student, newly enriched with the gifts of the Holy Spirit, who wonders about the gifts of healing and whether they make the completion of his medical training unnecessary. For all such readers something rather more down to earth is needed.

The subtitle of my book is 'A doctor investigates'. Why make this point? What special insights can a medical man have on this topic? Two at least.

1. The doctor is going to be harder to convince. Medicine as a discipline is built on a foundation of sciences: and Ian Ramsey maintains that the scientist is bound, as a condition of using scientific words, to exclude 'miracle' from the start. The sciences of physiology: how the body functions in health; and of pathology: how it is affected by, and responds to disease, form the very bases of our medical practice day in, day out. So while miraculous healing may be of some interest to everybody, parishioner or priest, it is a crucial subject for the doctor, striking as it does at the very foundation of professional life. He or she therefore needs much better evidence than would satisfy other people. We look for proof, for cast-iron evidence not susceptible to other explanation. While this degree of evidence can rarely be produced I have tried and, in my first (1.1) and last (10.4) Case Records, at least, believe I have succeeded.

2. Contrariwise the doctor is going to find it easier to believe. Medicine, unlike dogma, is always rapidly changing. When I studied physiology as a newly demobbed airman the function of the thymus, which proves to be central to our defence against disease, was unknown. Pathology has changed since then: the auto-immune diseases were unrecognised as

such. And of course therapeutics has altered out of all recognition. In wartime Bengal I was sometimes on duty in the pharmacy of RAF sick quarters preparing large bottles of mixtures containing up to half a dozen ingredients. Only a few years later my Professor of Therapeutics would say that such elegantly prescribed and attractively packaged medicines were best emptied down the drain. At the time penicillin was a curiosity I had read about in a copy of *Reader's Digest*. All this is utterly changed. So the doctor accustomed to constant reappraisal, and to abandoning old beliefs for new knowledge, is better prepared to accept the sort of evidence that I am presenting than the man whose views are more fixed.

There have been two main stimuli to the preparation of this book. Some years ago a study group of the Christian Medical Fellowship, aware of the isolated cases of healing that were brought to the attention of doctors, and of increasing interest in claims for the charismata, looked for evidence from several sources. They knew that one of the founders of the CMF, Professor Rendle Short of Bristol, had looked for years for cases but with meagre success. They also reviewed the literature available, such as the work of Dr Louis Rose who had searched for evidence of faith cures and eventually (in 1968) confessed that: 'I have yet to find one "miracle cure"; and without that (or alternatively, massive statistics which others must provide) I cannot be convinced of the efficacy of what is commonly called faith healing.'[2] Accordingly, among others, I received a letter in November 1976 from the CMF secretary, Dr Douglas Johnson (to whom, perhaps more than any other colleague, Christian doctors owe a debt), which concluded: 'Do you know of any services where instead of just popular descriptions, there is anything like Case papers, showing the true nature of a diagnosis before the claimed healing and, if possible, Case papers or some certainty from medical observers that the change was lasting?' The study group's report, *Some Thoughts on Faith Healing*,[3] edited by Vincent Edmunds and Gordon Scorer, was unable to reach any very firm conclusions. I am sorry, DJ, that it has taken me a decade to get round to it, but here at last is, if not a series from one centre, at least a sizable collection of Case Records.

The second influence, although more esoteric, provided the vital nudge. It will become evident that I have a great interest in seventh-century Anglo-Saxon Northumbria. Out of this arose the topic of my presidential address to the Newcastle and Northern Counties Medical Society, 'Maternity, medicine and miracle in the Golden Age', a revised version of which has appeared in the *British Medical Journal.*[4] And the interest aroused by that article stimulated the invitation to write the book.

Among the criticisms which may be levelled against me are two from opposite sides, both concerned with the same factor: my dependence on case histories.

On the medical side are those who will snort, 'It's anecdotal'. For the benefit of readers outside my profession I should explain that 'anecdotal' is the derisory adjective applied to any case-history that is used to support an argument with which the listener does not agree. There are two responses I would like to make: first that until the twentieth century all medical knowledge was based on such anecdotal experience. Our predecessors, construing the corpus of medical knowledge from the dawn of history, worked on that foundation: men like Munro Kerr whose *Operative Obstetrics* (1908)[5] is the most valued work on my medical shelves and is still in print. This textbook is liberally sprinkled with anecdotes inserted by the author, and added to by later editors. It is upon the shoulders of such giants that we stand. The mind boggles at the modern preferred alternative, of formulating an experiment to test the efficacy of prayer for healing. For example, should we pray for alternate patients to the God and Father of our Lord Jesus Christ; and to C. S. Lewis's Tash? But that would not do, for to be acceptable we would have to make the study double-blind, so that we did not know to which of them we were praying. It is fun trying to construct the experiment (and in fact statistics have been published of improved plant-growth after prayer)[6] but I am not convinced that it would be a very useful or relevant exercise.

On the opposite side some Christians, similarly, will object to a study based on case histories rather than biblical passages. As Edmunds and Scorer wisely point out, 'We tend to take it for granted that the Bible will present us with a clearly definitive statement on such matters as this, which will leave no doubt about what the original writers intended to convey.' However, as they go on to show, interpretation by biblical scholars leads to a contrariety of opinions.[7] By basing their beliefs solely on Scripture different scholars – equally devout, equally sincere, equally able – have come up with mutually incompatible results. From the impeccable exegesis of one of them it clearly follows that physical healing will be granted to anyone who claims it by faith: but in all honesty it often does not happen like that. From the equally careful exegesis of another it follows that the gifts of the Spirit, such as healing, are not given today: but they are; intellectual honesty demands that verdict. The scholars' logically inevitable results do not follow. Eddie Askew[8] quotes someone as saying, 'God to me is a verb, not a noun.' That is relevant here. For by 'comparing Scripture with Scripture', but forgetting also to look out of the window at what God is actually doing, white is proved to be black, and black white. (When dealing with sacred data it is so easy to slip into the error of imagining that our reasoning also is sacrosanct.) If facts do not fit, then facts have to be discarded; and truth is the ultimate casualty. While unintentional this conclusion inevitably follows that approach, which must therefore logically be wrong.

In view of the unsatisfactory nature of the extensive literature what choice did I have but to take a different starting point?

'What saith the Scriptures?' while a vital point which we must tackle, is not the first question to ask. We should have known that, for it is not the approach found in Scripture: understanding arises out of divine deeds, not vice versa. In the Old Testament period each generation of Israelites got to know their God by what he had done: in fact they had to learn it by heart. At the festival of the first-fruits each had to go to the priest and recall God's deeds 'the Lord heard our voice . . . the Lord brought us out of Egypt . . . He brought us to this place and gave us this land. . .' (Deut. 26:7–9 NIV). They were encouraged with constant reminders. Joshua 4:6–7 must have worked out something like this. 'Look, kids, we'll take a picnic and pop down to the west bank of the Jordan this afternoon, because I want to show you the twelve great stones our ancestors lifted out of the bed of the river when God dried it up for them to cross: that will show better than anything I can say what a great God we've got.' The other nations learned about God the same way: to the unbelieving King Cyrus God said, 'I will go before you . . . I will break down gates of bronze . . . I will give you . . . so that you may know that I am the Lord' (Isa. 45:2–3 NIV).

In the New Testament we read of the ecclesiastical authorities of the day sitting round to argue with Jesus. During this session he healed the paralysed man. Our Lord turned on the critical Pharisees with: 'that you may know that the Son of Man has authority on earth to forgive sins', then, swinging round to the patient, 'get up, take your mat and go home' (Luke 5:24 NIV).

With hindsight we can so easily rubbish the Pharisees and members of the Sanhedrin, forgetting that there were good men among them, Nicodemus for one. Spare a thought for their problems. They had a difficult job keeping the faith of Israel alive in the presence of the Roman occupying forces; and even more dangerous was the pervasive influence of Hellenistic ideas. So they had to be vigilant to guard sound doctrine. They had not got a clue – how could they – that they were living in a new age of God's activity, that the calendar had turned from Before Christ to Anno Domini. They had dedicated their lives to a study of Scripture and identified a particularly important touchstone: Sabbath-keeping. Therefore founding their belief on inspired Scripture they were logical in adopting a highly critical attitude towards this theologically untrained upstart from the provinces. Confronted with a man who claimed to have been given his

6

sight they looked for logical explanations; wrong diagnosis? wrong man? 'Well, even if we have to accept the phenomenon we can't change our stand: this healer has got to be a sinner: because he offends against our scripturally based criteria.' And they believed that charge, it was not trumped up. We can understand their real problem, for it is that of some present-day Christians, one of whom wrote in 1985:[9] 'Biblical evangelicalism, which stresses the Word alone and believes in the standing miracle of the new birth and in mighty acts of providence, rejects the contemporary signs and revelations as not being from God, however remarkable they may appear to be.' Our answer is the same as the blind man's cured by our Lord: 'Whereas I was blind, now I see. . . Here is a marvel! You do not know where he comes from and yet he opened my eyes . . . if this man were not from God he could do nothing' (John 9:25, 30, 33 RSV).

Again when John the Baptist sent messengers to ask if Jesus was indeed the Messiah, our Lord did not reply with a string of scriptural references, but by pointing to a series of cases of miraculous healings which meshed into OT prophecy (Matt. 11:2–6 with Isa. 35:5–6). Therefore I am on sure ground in taking as the foundation of my book a series of miraculous healings which mesh into NT prophecies, which we shall look into in detail. In other words I am following the biblical pattern in first recording what God is doing, and then deducing principles. Some may warn that starting with experience risks confusion, for there are patients apparently miraculously healed through non-Christian, or even satanic practitioners. But as already stated my case is confined to healing following prayer to God offered by Christians, defining that term by the sufficient biblical, solid and unnegotiable christological criteria found in Romans 10:9: 'That if you confess with your mouth, "Jesus is Lord," and believe in your heart that God raised him from the dead, you will be saved' (NIV); and 1 John 4:2–3:

This is how you can recognise the Spirit of God: Every spirit that acknowledges that Jesus Christ has come in the flesh is from God, but every spirit that does not acknowledge Jesus is not from God. This is the spirit of the antichrist, which you have heard is coming and even now is already in the world. (NIV)

When I was practising my speciality in Mbale hospital in eastern Uganda, on one Sunday evening a month the Bishop and Dean of St Andrew's Cathedral allowed me to conduct the service after the Presbyterian order. So when the time came for us to leave and friends asked what I planned to do on return to Britain, I would reply jokingly, 'I'm planning to work in the hinterland between obstetrics and theology.' At least I thought I was joking, unaware that the Abortion Act with its major moral problems, and the charismatic renewal with its explosion of interest in healing, were just over the horizon.

Ian Ramsey writes,[10] 'Healing miracles (are) a salient topic on the frontier between religion and medicine'; and M. A. H. Melinsky goes on,[11] 'Whoever sets sail to explore the subject of miracles risks shipwreck on a variety of shoals. He must face major difficulties of theology, philosophy, history and science.' It is a tall order, especially for a full-time obstetrician and gynaecologist, however co-operative his friends and librarians may be, who has to rely largely on his own bookshelves. I only ask that those trained in the disciplines Melinsky has enumerated will be understanding.

1. I. Ramsey, 'Miracles: an exercise in logical mapwork', in *Miracles and the Resurrection*. London, SPCK 1964.
2. L. Rose, *Faith Healing*, qu. in V. Edmunds and C. G. Scorer (eds), *Some Thoughts on Faith Healing*, 3rd rev. edn (London, CMF 1979), pp. 61–2.
3. Edmunds and Scorer. See n. 2.
4. R. F. R. Gardner, 'Miracles of healing in Anglo-Celtic Northumbria as recorded by the Venerable Bede and his contemporaries: a reappraisal in the light of twentieth-century experience', in *British Medical Journal*, 287 (1983), pp. 1927–33.
5. Munro Kerr, *Operative Obstetrics*, 10th edn, ed. P. R. Myerscough. London, Baillière, Tindall and Cox, 1981.

6. qu. in F. McNutt, *Healing* (Notre Dame, Ave Maria Press 1974), pp. 31–2.
7. Edmunds and Scorer, p. 15.
8. *Disguises of Love: meditations and prayers by Eddie Askew* (London, Leprosy Mission 1983), p. 70.
9. V. Budgen, *The Charismatics and the Word of God* (Welwyn, Evangelical Press 1985), p. 220.
10. I. Ramsey, in introd. to M. A. H. Melinsky, *Healing Miracles*. London, Mowbray 1968.
11. Melinsky, p. 1.

1

Miracles:
a possibility worth investigating?

One Friday evening in the early 1970s I found myself on my knees examining a woman's ankle. While nowadays, as a gynaecologist, I am not concerned with lesions in that part of the body, I had had some experience of chronic leg ulcers from my days as a medical missionary: in Nigeria they are common, usually due to hoeing injuries caused by iron machetes. They are difficult to heal whatever the medical treatment.

CASE RECORD 1.1

The story is of a large varicose ulcer above the right ankle, present for many years. Each morning the dressing was soaked with pus. The patient, who was captain in the Girls' Brigade in our church, had at last been told by her doctor that such physical activity must be given up if there was to be any hope of the ulcer healing. She was loath to abandon this Christian service, so prayer was asked for healing in the monthly prayer meeting. Two doctors were present, one of whom mentioned after examining the ankle that if it were to heal skin-grafting would be necessary. The pastor asked one of the ladies present to join him in laying hands on the patient, and in prayer for healing.

By next morning almost the whole ulcer had dried up with healthy skin covering, but one corner continued to exude pus. A week later one of the young lieutenants in the Girls' Brigade called on the pastor and with some embarrassment told him that she felt she should have joined in prayer for the patient. They immediately called on her, the girl laid hands on the area and prayed. Healing thereupon became complete.

All this had happened the previous month in my absence. Now along with another practitioner I examined the ankle. It was some 4 cm narrower than the other one, evidence of the tissue destruction which had taken place, but there was no evidence of the former varicose eczema, and the ulcer was replaced by the healthiest skin on the whole leg.

At the time, which is described by Don Bridge and David Phypers in *More than Tongues can Tell*,[1] we were seeing so many new things happening in the congregation that this was taken more or less in our stride. It is only in retrospect that the true significance of that occasion in Crosslea Avenue, Sunderland, becomes clear.

Miracles do not happen. That is almost universally accepted in the educated world. What evidence would be needed to shake this view? The philosopher David Hume[2] put the issue starkly two hundred years ago when he wrote:

> There is not to be found in all history any miracle attested by a sufficient number of men of unquestionably good sense, education and learning, as to be secure against all delusions in themselves: of such undoubted integrity to place them beyond all suspicion of any design to deceive others, of such credit and reputation in the eyes of mankind as to have a good deal to lose in case of being detected in a falsehood: and at the same time attesting facts performed in a public manner, and in so celebrated a part of the world, as to render detection unavoidable.

Well, Mr Hume: several medical practitioners involved; in the home of a senior lecturer in pharmacy; in a large town in England – will that satisfy your criteria?

There is however another question. Are miracles the sort of facts which are susceptible to normal rules of evidence? Benedicta Ward, a sympathetic historian and member of a religious order, in her study, *Miracles and the Mediaeval Mind*,[3]

11

comments that the historian has rarely found first-hand evidence in his own time. For herself, 'it will seem that I have avoided a direct answer to the question of whether miracles "really" happen. It seems to me that such a question is beyond the scope of a historical work: it belongs to theology and especially to philosophy.' Similarly, in *Miracle in the Early Christian World*,[4] Howard Clark Kee writes: 'But is it sufficient to ask concerning miracle – or any other phenomenon from the ancient world – "Did it really happen"? The hermeneutically prior and far more important question is, "What did the ancient writer who reported the event understand to have occurred?" '

This cautious approach, typical of almost all scholarly writing, will not do for us, doctor or patient, at the crunch. In this study I am looking at the experience of our own time, employing both scientific and theological reasoning, and above all I do not propose to avoid the question whether these things really happen. Leg ulcers and ovarian cysts are not states of mind; or our medical care and surgical procedures are unfounded. This is not esoteric discussion, we are in a 'need to know' situation.

But first, what do we mean by 'miracle'? It proves difficult to pin down but some examples will help towards a definition.

Benedicta Ward draws attention to a useful example from a twelfth-century account of the escape of the Empress Matilda from beleaguered Oxford. The contemporary writer William of Malmesbury recorded:[5] 'It is undoubtedly one of God's manifest miracles.' Yet having used that phrase he goes on with a down-to-earth explanation of its happening owing to the desertion of many of the besiegers and the lessened vigilance of the others. Why then did he call it 'a manifest miracle'? Probably because William thought it an edifying instance of God manifest in affairs. Such an explanation would fit in well with Jim Packer's suggested definition, 'A miracle is a particular kind of physical event having spiritual significance and value.'[6]

But there is a snag. Does not such a definition include all

answers to prayer? Are we to call them all miracles? And if so, do we not emasculate the term?

'Give us this day our daily bread', we pray, as taught by Jesus. When is the answer miraculous? Compare the following accounts from France and from Bristol.

In the early nineteenth century the Curé of Ars[7] ran a home for orphan girls. On one occasion the miller failed to return the ground flour and there was only enough for two loaves for eighty children. Nevertheless the curé told the cook to start preparations and mix the yeast as usual.

> The next day [reported Jeanne-Marie Chaney] as I kneaded, the dough rose under my hands; I could not pour in water fast enough. The more I poured the more the dough swelled and thickened – so much so that in a few minutes the trough was quite full. . . We made the usual batch of ten large loaves of 20 to 22 pounds apiece – and with a handful of flour – as much as we were accustomed to make with a whole sackful.

Another time there was no bread and neither corn flour nor money. The curé sent for the superior of the house and said to her with a very full heart, 'We shall have to send away our poor children since we cannot find food for them.' But before proceeding to this extremity he went to look in the granary once more: it was full. The miller was sent for and as he filled his sacks declared that he had never handled such fine wheat. Very properly the curé's assistant, who recorded these incidents, terms them 'miracles'.

Later the same century in Bristol orphan homes were run by George Müller. The title of his *Autobiography: or, a million and a half in answer to prayer*,[8] makes it clear that he too relied on God to supply their needs. A number of times the food supply ran out and Müller and his fellow-workers had to pray urgently. Once there was not a halfpenny left to buy food for the next day. Another time there was food for the midday meal but nothing for the evening. Yet again, except for potatoes, there was nothing for a meal due in three hours. Each time a cheque arrived in the post or someone called with money in time for food to be bought and prepared. The orphans never went hungry. But the word 'miracle' is not employed.

These two examples help towards a definition. In the Bristol incidents human intermediaries were involved. Any single incident could have been an example of what is called 'a lucky coincidence' such as we all experience occasionally. But happening as they did time after time, following – or sometimes even during – prayer for the specific need, that explanation cannot be sustained. It is clear that God was behind the supply but employing means which were unexceptional by their nature. But in the Ars cases there was no human intermediary. In human experience flour never multiples. There is no logical explanation available apart from the intervention of God. Let us then use that criterion in our definition of 'miracle'.

The distinction between answer-to-pray and miracle is often difficult in cases of healing. To the cosmic watchers (Heb. 12:1) it is doubtless unreal: they will see all as gracious activity by a loving God. In our ordinary life in the body of Christ it is also probably not worth making; but for the purpose of this study we must try to distinguish: I shall detail answer-to-prayer healings but will not number them or give them the status of Case Records. As an example let me report the following medical history:

A woman in her eighties was admitted to a District General Hospital late in 1985 with acute abdominal pain. She had an emergency operation, after which her relatives were given to understand that the bowel was gangrenous but that she had not been fit enough for anything to be done. She was returned to the ward, and obviously the prognosis was considered bleak. Much prayer was offered for her.

Two days later she had improved to a surprising extent, and the surgeon tentatively raised the question of further surgery with her daughter-in-law (from whom I learned the story). Permission having with some trepidation been given, the surgeon had her moved to theatre within the

14

hour, only to come out to her waiting kin with the marvellous news that the bowel was perfectly healthy.

He has provided me with further information. His understanding is that the patient had had a cardiovascular episode resulting in a drop in blood pressure as a result of which the blood flow to her bowel was compromised: it was at that stage that the first operation was performed. As her condition improved, and her blood pressure rose to normal levels, perfusion (flushing) of the bowel-wall resumed with the satisfactory results discovered at the second operation.

It is clear to me that the happy result was a surprise to the doctors, for none of us would willingly subject a poor-risk patient to the hazards of a second major abdominal procedure unless we expected to tackle some dire condition which justified the considerable anaesthetic and operative risks. Without discounting medical and nursing care this excellent result can therefore be ascribed to an answer to prayer. However as the reversal of the pathological process is susceptible to medical explanation, a definition of 'miracle' is excluded.

By contrast I consider Case Record 1.2 (see p. 20) to be a miracle for a number of reasons but principally because the scotoma (scar in the eye), which in medical experience never disappears, did just that.

It can with justice be said that all healing is divine. As Ambroise Paré the sixteenth-century Huguenot royal surgeon put it, 'I bind the wounds, and God heals them.' However that is not what we are thinking about. To lend meaning to our study we are regarding healing miracles as those cures for which, apart from the intervention of God, there is no logical explanation. The consideration of alternative explanations is the task of Chapter 2.

Having said all that, are miracles possible? If not we are wasting our time. C. S. Lewis[9] has made the point that if the end of the world appeared in all the literal trappings of the apocalypse, if the modern materialist saw with his own eyes the heavens rolled up and the great white throne appearing, if he had the sensation of being himself thrown into the Lake of Fire, he would continue forever, in the lake itself, to regard his experience as an illusion and find the explanation in psychoanalysis or cerebral pathology. Everything, in a word, depends on our presuppositions.

It is mere confusion of thought to suppose that advancing scientific knowledge makes it harder to accept miracles, for we always knew they were contrary to the natural course of events. Testimony to the miraculous was as unacceptable to Plato in classical Greece or to the educated person in the Roman Empire as it is to their twentieth-century counterparts. From the advance of science we have learnt some of the rules by which nature works. Those of us who believe in miracles are not denying the laws of nature, which are merely descriptions of our observations: therefore they cannot be 'broken'; new facts irreconcilable with current 'laws of nature' merely indicate that they will have to be reframed. But a purely secular framework may prove inadequate. With Lewis we believe that nature as we know it is only a part, perhaps a very small part, of the *imperium* ruled by God. So it is a mistake to think that a disturbance in the formulae of terrestrial nature would constitute a breach of the living rule whereby God works. If miracles do occur then we may be sure that not to have wrought them would be the real inconsistency.

In some cases God seems merely to turn the knob to 'fast-run'. At Cana (John 2:1–10) the God who year by year turns water into wine through vines short-circuited the process, making wine in a moment. Just so the Lord who one day will turn our battered worn-out bodies into the likeness of Christ's resurrection body, sometimes does his renewing work locally and temporarily by a healing miracle.

These miracles are different from the so-called 'miracle stories' of which the Middle Ages were full: fairy-tale wonders, prodigies, literary decorations of the most improbable kinds such as the tale of the woman of Wye[10] who was cured when she drank water from a fountain that had been blessed by an abbot. She at once vomited two large black toads which turned into two huge black dogs and then into asses. Then she was sprinkled with water from the fountain whereupon the creatures ascended into the sky leaving a bad smell. Is that to be ranked a miracle? Such stories may be fun, like those of ships turned into goddesses or beasts into men, but the least suspicion that they might be true could turn the fun into nightmare, for they would show that nature was being invaded by an alien power.

In contrast Christian miracles are not wonders to make people gawk but are congruent and appropriate, signs that the creator God has not lost his touch or his concern. If we accept that there is a God we cannot, in advance, claim that nature is safe from his intervention.

But granted this, there is another problem. Are not miracles unfair? After I had recounted one or two of these case histories in a radio interview a listener wrote to the BBC: 'If God has the power which miracles purport to demonstrate, why does he not use it to put the world to rights? Why healing and not food? Why heal a child in Newcastle upon Tyne and leave millions of children starving in the third world?' It is a problem that worries believers too. Our Lord, while living in Palestine, visited the Pool of Bethesda where there was a multitude of invalids, blind, lame and paralysed. He healed one man and left the rest. Why? The eighteenth-century deist Thomas Woolston was blunt: 'If he could not cure them, there's an end of his power of miracles; and if he would not, it was want of mercy and compassion in him.'[11]

Sixty years ago an episcopal critic[12] of healing missions drew attention to those who wonder secretly at God's apparent favouritism:

Suffering saddens and perplexes, but it does not alienate us, for under the bitter covenant of pain we all must live and He suffers with us; but the partiality of favouritism, which grants exemption from the general curse, not on any intelligible principle or in the service of any adequate cause, but by mere caprice at this shrine, or at that man's hands,

17

alarms and revolts us. Not the credit of the churches, but the character of God is the issue at stake in this controversy, 'Shall not the Judge of all the earth do right?'

It is obvious that he thought the last sentence settled this issue; but had he turned the coin and looked at the question of unexplained tragedy and suffering he would have realised that our questionings are not so neatly set at rest.

It is a problem of the activity of God which Jesus himself recognised. On one occasion (Mark 7:24–30) in response to the pleadings of a Lebanese woman (which he granted) he made the point that the blessings were for the Jews. He does not baulk at the apparently arbitrary behaviour of God, almost going out of his way to remind his Jewish listeners (Luke 4:25–7) that although there were many needy widows in Israel in the days of Elijah the prophet he was sent as a miraculous supplier of food only to a non-Jewish widow in Sidon; and again that although there were many Jewish lepers in the days of Elisha, that prophet healed only Naaman – a Syrian (see p. 107).

Yes, it does not seem fair. Must God be arraigned on a charge of favouritism? In my reading today (Rom. 9) Paul tackles the question head-on in an important passage for our own tortured century. Why should God show favour to Jacob rather than Esau while they were still twins in the womb? Now do we conclude that God is monstrously unfair? Never! 'For he says to Moses, "I will have mercy on whom I have mercy, and I will have compassion on whom I have compassion" ' (NIV). It is obviously not a question of human will or human effort, but of divine mercy. God chose the younger twin Jacob as heir of the promises, and rejected the elder sib Esau, in order to show that his salvation rests on his promise alone, and not on natural order or any similar prerogative. Dean Alford[13] paraphrases God's own comment on the choice as: 'Whenever I have mercy on any it shall be pure mercy, no human desert contributing.' In C. H. Dodd's phrase,[14] 'This is indeed the quality of mercy. If it counts deserts it is not mercy.' But we are still not satisfied.

18

Is it not inevitable that from the highest pinnacle of human faith there should ring out the mad questioning cry, 'Is not such a God unrighteous?' Yes, is He not indeed a capricious, spiteful demon, seeking to make fools of us all? Does He not rebel against the laws of righteousness which He ought to obey?

These questions were directed to the German Church, so soon to suffer under the Nazi heel, by Karl Barth in his *Commentary on the Epistle to the Romans*.[15] But he concludes with the affirmation and reassurance that 'God would not be God were He not liable to such accusations'. We should be content to settle for God's words to Isaiah (55:8–9 NEB): 'For my thoughts are not your thoughts, and your ways are not my ways. This is the very word of the Lord. For as the heavens are higher than the earth, so are my ways higher than your ways and my thoughts than your thoughts.'

But to the obvious riposte, why not mercy for everyone, today, the answer is: because mankind has proclaimed UDI. That unilateral declaration of independence means that the royal rule is refused. As long as mankind flaunts his independence of God, God is not free to act for his good. But he is working on it. The coming of our Lord to Bethlehem and his death on the cross were the essential steps to our reconciliation. When that is achieved, when Christ is King, all suffering will be gone and every need abundantly satisfied. For the moment, present-day miracles – few though they seem but more numerous than we know – are the first drips announcing the thaw, the first snowdrops heralding the spring, the first proclamations of the approach of the King who will destroy evil and disease and want, and set up his kingdom.

If we accept that miracles are philosophically reasonable, we can proceed to the central question: do they occur in the field of healing?

In an endeavour to answer that question by presenting a series of medical histories I have deliberately confined myself to cases where I have been able to check the history, as I do in clinical practice, by reference to the personal reports and records of professional colleagues. I have selected particular Case Records for which I believe, on the evidence I would look for in my own discipline, that divine intervention in the course of the disease is the only logical explanation.

Let us look at one of these. A mutual medical friend put me in touch with the patient, who then sent me her own account and let me see the pathological reports and the hospital discharge letter.

CASE RECORD 1.2

A young trainee General Practitioner in North Wales went to visit her pastor and his wife one evening in January 1975. She was obviously not well and they prevailed on her to stay overnight in the manse. This was indeed providential for next morning they found her unconscious. She was admitted moribund (at the point of death) to hospital with meningococcal septicaemia and meningitis (Waterhouse-Friderichsen syndrome). No such case had ever survived in that hospital.

That evening groups praying for her in Rhyl, Llandudno, Caernarfon and Bangor, independently but simultaneously, believed that their request that she might be healed with no residual disability had been granted. At the same time, 8.30 p.m., there was a sudden improvement in her condition, although it was four days before she regained consciousness. Physicians were unable to explain why her chest x-ray films, which had shown extensive left-sided pneumonia with collapse of the middle lobe, could, forty-eight hours later, show a normal chest.

The ophthalmologist saw and photographed a scar (central scotoma) in the left eye caused by intra-ocular haemorrhage affecting the macula – a vital part of the visual apparatus. He assured the patient that there was permanent blindness in that eye. Her faith that God had promised her she would be made 'every whit whole' (John 7:23 av) was not unreasonably met with his, 'You have got to face medical facts.' When she did in fact develop perfect vision in that eye and no residual disease could be found, he was understandably unable to offer any explanation, and could only say, 'Do you realise that you are unique?'

The four consultants who saw her on admission to hospital remain confident of their initial diagnosis. She is shown at post-graduate medical meetings as 'The one that got away.'

This sort of evidence is not usually met with by the modern scholar. But we can see he would respond by comparing his reaction with that of the medieval historian, who is unable to avoid the number of miraculous stories embedded in his primary sources. Where that source is such a respected reporter as Bede, today's historian has a problem. Meyveart[16] spells this out: 'The modern scholar is above believing in miracles; in fact from his point of view "scholarship" and "belief in miracles" are mutually exclusive terms. He will therefore seek to deal with the miraculous element in Bede's works . . . in a sophisticated way'. So the scholar tries to find a way out of his dilemma. He suggests that the reporter of miraculous healings held a different view of truth or of facts; that what mattered was the purpose of the report rather than its content – anything but tackle the question, was the person healed as stated? For obviously that possibility cannot be entertained if intellectual suicide is to be avoided.

This is an area which Bonser[17] rightly identifies as 'a dangerous field placed between theology and medicine, that no one has dared thoroughly to explore'. As we make this exploration let me state that the Case Records are, to the best of my ability, medically accurate, and the facts as stated. I suggest that intellectual honesty demands that we face them.

1. D. Bridge and D. Phypers, *More than Tongues Can Tell.* London, Hodder & Stoughton 1982.
2. D. Hume, *An Enquiry Concerning Human Understanding*, qu. in H. C. Kee,

Miracle in the Early Christian World: a study in sociohistorical method (New Haven and London, Yale 1983), pp. 11–12.

3. B. Ward, *Miracles and the Mediaeval Mind.* London, Scolar Press 1982.
4. H. C. Kee. See n. 2.
5. William of Malmesbury, *Chronicles of the Kings of England,* ed. J. A. Giles (London, Bohn 1847), p. 535.
6. J. Packer, qu. in J. P. Baker, *Salvation and Wholeness* (London, Fountain Trust 1973), n. 19.
7. See A. Monnin, *The Curé d'Ars.* London, Sands n.d.; and H. Ghéon, *The Secret of the Curé d'Ars.* London, Sheed & Ward 1952.
8. G. Müller, *Autobiography; or, a million and a half in answer to prayer.* London, Nisbet 1914.
9. C. S. Lewis, *Miracles: a preliminary study.* London, Bles 1947.
10. Robert of Hoveden, qu. in B. Ward, 'Miracles and history: a reconsideration of the miracle stories used by Bede', in *Famulus Christi: essays in commemoration of the 13th centenary of the birth of the Venerable Bede,* ed. G. Bonner (London, SPCK 1976), pp. 70–7.
11. T. Woolston, qu. in C. Brown, *Miracles and the Critical Mind.* Exeter, Paternoster; and Grand Rapids, W. B. Eerdmans 1984.
12. H. H. Henson, *Notes on Spiritual Healing* (London, Williams & Norgate 1925), pp. 196–7.
13. H. Alford, *The Greek Testament* (1849), rev. E. F. Harrison. Chicago, Moody Press 1958.
14. C. H. Dodd, *The Epistle to the Romans.* London, Hodder & Stoughton 1932.
15. K. Barth, *Commentary on the Epistle to the Romans* (1921), Eng. tr. E. C. Hoskyns. London, OUP 1933.
16. P. Meyveart, 'Bede the scholar', in *Famulus Christi.* See n. 10.
17. W. Bonser, 'The medical background of Anglo-Saxon England', *Wellcome Historical Medical Library* (1963).

2

Miracles:
is some other explanation possible?

If we are to make assertions for miracles, proclaiming them signs of God's power, we must be meticulous in excluding cases in which some other cause is more likely. Such an examination of the evidence is not dishonouring to God but is essential 'because of the truth, which lives in us and will be with us for ever' (2 John 2 NIV). It involves going into the histories in detail. I read accounts of 'miraculous healings' in the Christian press which I can immediately dismiss because they fit more readily into other categories. It may be a pity to do so, for no doubt some of them are in fact miracles, but without more information how am I to be persuaded? And this accords with Martyn Lloyd-Jones's emphasis, 'we must still continue to maintain our healthy sceptical and critical attitude to everything that is reported to us'.[1] It is for that reason that I make no apology for giving as full details as possible, even if they are technical and sometimes gory, for without them my claim of 'miracle' could be shrugged off. The first group to be excluded are cases in which the cure could fit in with the natural processes of the body.

Physiological Process?

'It's a miracle!' One day while walking through the hospital I was hailed with this cry by the pastor of a local church. It transpired that he had just been to see one of his parishioners before her operation, only to find that she was being sent home, the hysterectomy no longer necessary. I did not have beds in that ward but went up at once to quiz the sister in charge. It turned out that the hysterectomy had been planned because of menorrhagia (heavy periods). The patient had been on a waiting list for more than a year. By the time that she was eventually admitted her periods had stopped, therefore the procedure was not needed. Her cure was in all probability purely physiological. Since then the same thing has happened to two of my own patients but, as far as I am aware, without prayer having been offered for them.

That is not to assert that there was no divine intervention in the case of the pastor's friend. It may be that her personal physiological clock was set so as not to reach the menopause for several more years, in which case her trouble would have continued – or hysterectomy have been necessary – if God had not intervened. We have no means of knowing. But we do know that menorrhagia is a condition he has dealt with before. Our medical predecessor Luke (8:43–8) records the day when Jesus, immediately after landing on the lakeshore, was being hustled off towards Jairus' home. En route he stopped to heal a woman of just this gynaecological problem.

Spontaneous Remission?

The second group will prove to be our biggest difficulty, for many diseases can, even if only on rare occasions, undergo remission.

An article in the *British Medical Journal*,[2] written by a general practitioner, describes the history of one of his patients who at the age of ten developed a cancer (a retro-peritoneal sarcoma), proven at operation but irremovable, and was sent home grossly anaemic, to die. The mass resolved spontaneously and in a few months she began to live a normal life. Eventually she married another of his patients and became the mother of three children. She was examined at the age of eighteen by two consultants from the Central Cancer Registry and was found to have no trace of the tumour. Now middle-aged she is still healthy.

In 1956 after a search of world literature Everson and Cole[3] found reports of 600 spontaneous remission cases, of which they considered only forty-seven worthy of investigation. Significant factors, in their view, were endocrine influences, unusual sensitivity to inadequate radiation or other therapy, fever and/or infection, interference with the nutrition of the tumour, and removal of the carcinogenic agent. A few years later Smithers[4] in his study of the subject concluded that ' "Spontaneous" tumour regression is a well authenticated natural phenomenon. Its study may lead us to a better understanding of the natural history of neoplastic disease which so commonly progresses but rarely regresses.'

In view of this, almost all miraculous healings can be shrugged off as spontaneous remissions. So does not this make our present investigation impossible? No, for in some cases such remission is inconceivable: Case Record 1.1 (p. 10), for example. But more important their time relationship to believing prayer in the name of the Lord Jesus places them in a different category. When we note this time relationship recurring again and again it would be unscientific to neglect or discount it.

The next record, which demonstrates this relationship, was brought to my notice by the family doctor in the case, and the professor who treated the child in hospital prepared the summary for me. Both are personally convinced that this is a case of God's miraculous intervention. As the summary is rather technical I preface it with a resumé in lay language.

CASE RECORD 2.1

Resumé. An eight-month-old boy developed progressive scarring of the lungs following an attack of measles. It did not respond to the only useful treatment, so he was allowed to go home, and his mother was told the outlook was hopeless. He was taken to a healing service and within days improved, and since then has never looked back.

Summary. This child was the second born to healthy parents.

He thrived for eight months, gaining weight consistently on the 75th percentile. In May 1977, at eight months, he developed measles from which he never made a full recovery. Over the next three months he gradually became more apathetic, anorexic, and dyspnoeic. He lost weight from 8.8 to 7.4 kg.

He was admitted to the Royal Victoria Infirmary, Newcastle upon Tyne, at eleven months, a wasted miserable little scrap, severely dyspnoeic at rest with marked lower costal and intercostal recession. Chest radiograph showed diffuse confluent mottling with a small right pneumothorax. He was treated initially with antibiotics to which there was no response and a definitive diagnosis of advancing fibrosing alveolitis was established by lung biopsy. He was treated for six weeks on high dosage cortico-steriods without improvement, and for a further six weeks on cortico-steroids combined with azathioprine, again without improvement. Blood-gas analyses over this period of three months showed progressive deterioration [PO_2 5.1 kPa at the end of this treatment].

At this point his mother was told that in as much as there had been no response whatever to conventional therapy it was thought the disease was likely to be progressive and the outlook was hopeless. He was discharged at this point on maintenance prednisolone.

(At the suggestion of the general practitioner who was aware that a nearby pentecostal pastor was preparing himself for a healing service, and on learning from the professor that he was agreeable, the child was taken to the service on 26 February 1978.)

Five days after the healing service he appeared very slightly happier and more ready to play. Two weeks later he was definitely a stronger, happier, more active child, able to pull himself up to stand for the first time in more than four months. From this point he made steady consistent progress as shown by his weight chart and successive blood analyses. [At 2 yrs 3 months PO_2 was 8.3 kPa and eight months later 10.5 kPa.] He has been followed since then and when last seen at the age of 5 years and 2 months he was a perfectly normal boy with weight just below the 50th percentile.

The professorial summary concludes: 'The prognosis of fibrosing alveolitis starting in the first year of life is almost uniformly fatal.' As already noted it is that word 'almost' which makes proof of miraculous healing very difficult. However it would require a considerable degree of scepticism to believe that this was a rare case of spontaneous remission, which happened by sheer coincidence at exactly the same time as a healing service. When additionally the other Case Records are considered, the likelihood of all these cures being associated by mere chance with believing prayer must be astronomically remote.

Therapeutic Response?

In a third group, healing proves to have been due to the treatment given. For instance, Bede[5] records how Cuthbert when a boy had a swelling of the knee, as a result of which he could hardly walk at all. One day he was carried outside to lie in the sun. A horseman approached dressed in white and asked for hospitality. Cuthbert replied that he was only too ready to provide this but was pinned down by his knee, which no doctor anywhere had skill enough to cure. The horseman looked at it and said, 'Boil some wheaten flour in milk and bathe the tumour with it hot, and you will be healed.' This was done and in a few days the knee was cured. If we allow the seventh-century view that the horseman was an angel, then a miracle is involved, but the sensible treatment of hot poulticing does not deserve that classification.

Incorrect Diagnosis?

Medicine is not at the stage where certainty is always possible: it is not an exact science. In my fourth group, whereas in some cases recovery would have been miraculous had the disease initially suspected been present, it may not be unexpected in the light of the true diagnosis. In normal gynaecological practice I have occasionally had to tell relatives that I suspected cancer in their loved one and that major surgery was required; only to find, to our immense relief, that the tumour or cyst was benign. Return to full health in such cases is to be expected. Some examples of 'miraculous healing' published in popular Christian literature probably fall into this category: for instance, in the older books 'cancers' that have 'dropped out' are very likely cases of benign fibroma on a thin pedicle.

A real problem however exists, in view of the unexpected outcome, where the diagnosis may have been made retrospectively. My attention was drawn to the case of a child who, previously well, suddenly collapsed and within three days was in a neurosurgical unit. The parents were told that the x-rays suggested a large intracranial (within the skull) growth. A prayer-chain was activated (which involves each member immediately telephoning three others on the list, as a result of which many Christians can be mobilised to pray within the hour). Surgery was performed. My letter to the surgeon elicited this reply: 'We thought he had a brain tumour but the histology [the microscopic examination of the tissue in the laboratory afterwards] of the swollen cerebellum showed that he was simply suffering from cerebellar oedema of uncertain origin.' (The cerebellum is part of the brain; and oedema is fluid in the tissue.) It is, without a doubt, better to operate unnecessarily than take a chance and omit a potentially life-saving procedure. However I cannot help wondering if the neurosurgeon was too modest in his implication that the original diagnosis was mistaken. Was there in fact an intracranial tumour which the Lord graciously removed before the operation? We do not know, we cannot know. It would seem clear that the parents were justified in considering this an answer to prayer, although in the absence of clinical proof I cannot include it in the criteria of 'miracle'.

In orthopaedic conditions the problem is greater in view of

the well recognised entity of hysterical paralysis. I know of a woman who was almost wheelchair-bound until, during a service, sensation returned to her toes for the first time in many months. She recovered completely and has travelled extensively. However she is still seen from time to time for her diabetes, at the hospital where she had her initial treatment. On seeking confirmation of what her medical advisers at the time had called 'a miracle', I learnt that the original case-notes had been lost. The new folder refers to her previous 'hysterical paralysis', instead of the original diagnosis of diabetic neuropathy. Such a retrospective label provides an acceptable medical diagnosis. In almost any case of healing of a musculo-skeletal condition it can be a let-out which understandably the non-believer can grasp. It is however disappointing to find it used by believers. In a reference[6] to the healing of Margaret Macdonald (see p. 95) there is a footnote: 'No precise medical diagnosis at the time was given and hysteria has not been ruled out.' This may well be clinical caution, but if so should it not also have appeared against many of the cases miraculously cured by our Lord, which the same editors list on another page? In the case of Miss Macdonald I am not aware of any suggestion that her condition was skeletal, or that this escape clause was invoked by the bitter critics of the time, although they were quick to employ it in the case of Miss Fancourt (see p. 96) when she was cured of hip disease.

Psychosomatic?

Fifthly: we are all aware that our emotional state affects our bodily functions and health. Fear speeds up our heart rate, worry gives us indigestion; anxiety before some ordeal, such as an examination, makes us want to visit the loo frequently. For example, while I was nursing in the RAF I developed such a streaming cold with running nose and eyes that it was impossible to work and the medical officer told me to go off duty. However at that moment the telephone rang to tell me

I was posted home to Glasgow. This wonderful news was a real answer to prayer as it meant I could attend preparation classes for the pre-registration examinations for entry to medical school. It also meant that I could live at home. When I told the MO he commented, 'That will cure your cold.' It did immediately.

Most of us have had dramatic cures that are nothing to do with miracles but demonstrate the power of mind over matter. There is a group of 'psychosomatic' diseases, in which it is recognised that a principal factor is the effect of the psyche (mind) over the soma (body). The 'stress diseases' make up a major part of the work-load of general practice and include such conditions as peptic ulcer, asthma and migraine. It should not be assumed that it is a simple case of cause and effect; for example, that worry causes coronary thrombosis, for organic causes also operate, but the disease and worry tend to occur in the same people.

It is worth reminding ourselves that the person cured of a psychosomatic disease – whether by conventional means or miraculously – is as truly returned to health and has as much cause to be grateful as the person healed of a 'purely' organic condition. The distinction between these sorts of condition is in any case becoming blurred in medical thinking. We can no longer consider the healing of stress diseases as a second-rate success.

It has been shown that cancers will often spread rapidly in a patient who has recently been bereaved. Recent research has demonstrated that the five-year disease-free survival rate in women after diagnosis of breast cancer is statistically better in those whose attitude is to fight the disease than in those who stoically accept it, or who despair. We know something of the bodily mechanisms involved: both the hormonal and immunological defence mechanisms are eventually controlled by the fore-brain which is the seat of the emotions. Just as emotions are benefited by the loving care of Christians, acceptance into a warm-hearted fellowship, experience of sins forgiven, the realisation of welcome by a loving heavenly Father, and by the peace with God which allows acceptance of oneself; so there will inevitably be beneficial physical effects mediated through the psychoendocrine pathways. The patient who is healed by these or by biochemical alterations, is healed by mechanisms devised by our creator God and need not feel in any way less intimately cared for than those whose healing I classify miraculous. Such people tend to improve when they have good news. When they are prayed for, the surrounding love and the faith it evokes in them will cause an improvement in their symptoms. So we have the problem that if they are cured by God's miraculous power it is natural to ascribe the result merely to psychological improvement.

Colin Brown, in *Miracles and the Critical Mind*,[7] draws attention to the problem:

> Modern skeptics are perhaps less inclined to dismiss the historicity of all alleged miracles than were their counterparts in previous centuries. More is known today about psychosomatic factors in illness and healing. Modern medicine recognizes the phenomenon of remission. But in such cases the skeptic simply changes his categories. He grants the possible facticity of the report but at the price of denying its miraculous character.

The clinician will properly look for an explanation in terms of medicine, even if it is difficult to find. The Christian who does not rule out healing miracle will find a readier explanation. These points are illustrated in my next case.

A clergyman friend answered the telephone one day and heard one of his parishioners scream at him: 'I can see. I have looked your number up in the phone book myself.' Here is the story as recorded by the patient and filled out [bracketed] from hospital records supplied to me by one of the consultants responsible.

CASE RECORD 2.2

I am aged forty-two, a schoolteacher. On 18 March 1982 at 10.35 my eyesight was damaged by the malfunction of a photocopying machine. I had used the machine many times before, but on this occasion the result was a catastrophe. My eyes received the full force of the flash from the machine's 600 watt tungsten halogen lamp, and I was immediately stunned and blinded. My vision appeared to clear save for a greyish image of the flash which seemed to stay with me. However this continued for a number of days and I became aware that my vision was not improving and had greatly deteriorated as I could not read a newspaper or music, as I had been able to do in the past.

At that time my GP likened the incident to snow-blindness and said he thought the situation would improve. However by 2 April the position had not improved and I was referred to a consultant ophthalmologist and thence to a consultant neurologist.

[The eye itself was normal but there was a visual-field defect which they agreed was due to a lesion in the occipital cortex — that part of the brain responsible for vision. The neurologist commented: 'I think it quite possible that the intense flash from the photocopier has caused vasospasm in the left occipital cortex. Admittedly I have never heard of this complication but I can see no reason why it should not have occurred. The direction of exposure of the flash is quite appropriate for his present field defect.']

I was admitted to the Institute of Neurology, National Hospital, Queen's Square (London), on 22 April for two days of tests and observation. [CAT scan and other examinations failed to reveal any structural abnormality and no conclusive diagnosis of the cause of visual failure was reached. It was hoped that his symptoms would gradually improve. A possible diagnosis of basilar migraine was entertained. It was commented that the circumstances were particularly unusual.]

[The patient remained at home, off work, and had to be taken about by his wife.] Not long after my return life at home was suddenly transformed from despair into expectancy by a telephone call from a man I had never met. He explained that he was a minister from a local Methodist church. He had heard of my accident and was very sorry,

32

but he had met a man who was a Christian healer and I should arrange to go and see him. After some difficulty in contacting this man I eventually arranged to go and see him a few days later, on Sunday, 2 May. I knew then that something was about to happen, yet I had no idea what to expect. . .

Sunday came and I was driven by my wife to this man's home. When I went into the house I was filled with peace. I became relaxed in the presence of this total stranger and felt that I was no longer in despair, the situation was no longer hopeless. We spoke together, I told him of the accident, he told me of the healings that our Lord had channelled through him and we prayed together. There was no doubt in my mind that Jesus was in control of the situation. He laid hands on my head and over my eyes, but nothing dramatic happened, so I arranged to go again the next Friday.

[On 4 May, two days after that visit, the neurologist wrote to the patient's general practitioner, reporting: 'He could only read with difficulty. . . He asked about a further set of glasses but I think this should wait until the field defect has stabilised. He will probably need to wait for further improvement in his acuity before returning to work. I will see him again in two months' time.']

For those five days I waited, no longer anxious but filled with calm and reassuring confidence. On the Friday we arrived at about 4 p.m. and again prayed. But this time as soon as his hands were placed on my head I experienced a sensation of power in the form of a gently flowing electric current which flowed through his hands and through my skull. And when he placed his left hand over my left eye from behind, and his right hand diagonally opposite it at the back of my head I felt them joined in the middle, through my skull. I also became aware of the most vivid and beautiful colour blue that I have ever seen – even although my eyes were closed – and both the colour and the 'electric' sensation persisted until his hands were removed. At the same time I had also experienced the most amazing feeling of strength and warmth passing, in a tingling sensation, through my fingers and into my wrists and arms. At that moment I felt alive for the first time in weeks and I felt that I had been reborn into God's service and able to administer His healing power too.

By 5.30 that day I was reading telephone numbers from a directory with my worst affected eye with no difficulty at all whereas at lunchtime I had been unable to read the headlines in a national newspaper. On Monday, 10 May my GP confirmed that my vision had been restored, so that I returned to school on Wednesday, 12 May, gained promotion instead of a disability pension, and also started healing.

[The neurologist wrote to the GP: 'This man's vision, as you know, has returned completely to normal following a visit to a faith healer. He even says he has no need for glasses. I can find no defect. Presumably the relaxation from his visit to the faith healer has abolished persisting cerebral vasospasm in the occipital cortex.']

Although this may be the complete answer, we have seen that that explanation for the blindness was conjectural, and unique. What is clear is that some fifty days after the loss of vision it returned suddenly and completely during believing prayer. However what confirms to me the miraculous nature of the cure is that the patient's vision did not return to its pre-accident state – he had needed glasses for twelve years – but was restored better than before, so that he no longer needed them.

There are all sorts of faith healers, some of whom make no Christian claims, while in others the personality of the healer is stressed and seems to be of paramount importance. In the case reported such strictures are inappropriate. A booklet about the work of the healer in question mentions no name except that of our Lord. No exaggerated claims are made:

Jesus promised us that when we gather together in His name He will be with us. He also promised that whatsoever we ask in His name, this He will give us. So we know that He *is* present and always ready to answer our prayers. We come expecting to receive His compassion which may take effect in different ways. Some may receive instant healing – in others the process may be slow. Some may be healed in spirit and mind but not physically. We persevere in faith and hope, *surrendering ourselves entirely into God's hands*, relaxed, trusting and believing in His loving power and faithfulness.

From that healing centre I have been provided with other case histories but have not had the opportunity to follow them up.

Natural History of the Disease?

The sixth group of cases, of which we must be very careful, is where the natural history of the disease allows sudden improvements, such as periods of amelioration in the chronic stress diseases, or the reduction of a hernia. But even here we may, on occasion, see God obviously at work. The difference between miraculous and non-miraculous cure, of a very similar condition and in the same patient, is seen in our next case. In this instance I have not been able to refer to hospital or GP records, for as in so many third world situations there are none. When we arrived in northern Nigeria to join the staff of the Sudan United Mission hospital at Vom even the surgical in-patient records were kept on pieces of cardboard about 10×5 cm, which were not preserved. The following case has been furnished by a missionary nurse of that society and relates to a time after we had left Nigeria, when there was a remarkable spiritual awakening in the Church in Plateau Province. [My own comments are in brackets.]

CASE RECORD 2.3

It was in September 1977, I had been to Panyam and as I was driving back a verse I had read in *Daily Light*[8] that

35

morning kept coming to my mind: 'Sit still my daughter'.
I did say to the Lord, 'What's this about, as I'm sitting
still, driving?' but just went on. I was at home having a
very late meal when his wife came to say that Zha, my
cook, was not well. His hernia which he had had repaired
at Vom three or four years previously was bothering him.
By the time I saw him it was nearly dusk. I was truly
horrified to find Zha on a mat on the floor, cold and
clammy and terribly drawn looking. His pulse was slow
and irregular and a great lump was out on his right side
as big as my hand, hard and inflamed. He said it felt as
though all his inside was being pulled out. There was no
doubt that it was a severe strangulated hernia. I prayed
with him and went to find something stronger than the
codeine he had already had, and asked the Lord to help.
I think I got him something I use for patients in labour, I
hadn't much else. I went back and gave it to him and
waited. As there was no change or sign of anything
happening I felt I would have to try to get him to hospital.
The road was appalling [it involves crossing an unbridged
river, and climbing on earth roads up the plateau escarp-
ment, around three hours] and I had done it twice that
day, and I was not at all sure he would stand the journey.
I was sure he was going to die and leave a wife and several
children. As I got things ready and alerted someone to
travel with me I heard the verse I had heard all day: 'Sit
still my daughter.' I went for my *Daily Light* and read all
the verses. [The lead text emphasised on her mind proves
this to have been the reading for 4 September which
includes: 'Take heed and be quiet; fear not neither be
fainthearted.' 'Be still and know that I am God.' 'Said I
not unto thee, that if thou wouldst believe, thou shouldest
see the glory of God?' 'In returning and rest shall ye be
saved, in quietness and confidence shall be your strength.'
'Rest in the Lord and wait patiently for Him.' 'He that
believeth shall not make haste.']

I told the Lord I was sure He could heal but 'I can't

36

just sit still, but I'll waste some time and please if you are going to heal please do it quickly'. So I wasted some time going over the car tyre pressures, writing a letter to hospital, filling flasks, then Yohanna and I had a cup of coffee. I said, 'Lord, I must go. They'll not understand if I delay.' I walked to their house and there Zha was, warm, normal pulse, the lump completely gone. I had taken my *Daily Light* and Hausa Bible to read to Zha what the Lord had said, and I did. And we gave thanks and I went home just bursting with praise to·the Lord.

The next morning Zha came to work and looking as though nothing had happened, except that his eyes were sunken like someone who has had a severe shock. I gave him a few days off and crowds of folk came to greet him, and he was able to witness to them. Then he was asked to be an evangelist to a small church one and a half miles away which needed a strong Christian to counsel and encourage. I think there was a definite connection between the two.

In 1981 the other side gave trouble. A doctor was staying here and he tried to reduce the hernia, gave Zha a good hefty dose of sedatives and then said it would perhaps be wise to get him to hospital. The hernia was nothing like the size of the strangulation of 1977 on the other side. On the way to hospital Zha said, 'It has gone back.' So it had. I was in a bit of a dilemma, but we had coffee, and prayed, and came home. It was *not* like 1977, he still had pain and eventually went to Evangel hospital for an operation. It was weeks before he felt fit, and as he said it really wasn't a big one. How different!

As we see from the more minor 1981 incident, hernias do sometimes reduce spontaneously. The miraculous intervention of God in the 1977 incident can in my judgment only be ruled out if I am prepared to discount the preceding biblical .message as fiction or fraud. But the 1981 incident shows that the Lord does not always work in the same way.

37

A possible reason for this may be found in my correspondent's further comment:

> When Zha came out of the anaesthetic after his hernia repair an Alhaji [a devout Muslim who has made the pilgrimage to Mecca] came over to him in great excitement and asked where he had learnt Arabic. Zha said he did not know Arabic. But the Alhaji said that Zha had quoted verses from the Koran in Arabic as he was coming out of the anaesthetic.

They hope they were verses about the Lord, which the Koran does contain. Zha does speak in tongues and they still pray for this Alhaji.

Because of the various acceptable explanations: remission, psychosomatic factors and the rest; people feel happier to confine the subject to healing miracles, if they are compelled to consider the subject of miracle at all. It is wise therefore to remind ourselves that such miracles form only one group among many. Zha's speaking in Arabic, and the divine pre-warning to the missionary nurse to take the professionally unacceptable course of procrastination, are examples of the violation-of-nature sort of miracle, which also includes the multiplication of food in Chapter 1 (p. 13). Contemporary experience of this can be found from Mexico. René Laurentin, in *Miracles in El Paso?*[9] gives several incidents within the last ten years including, for example, the distribution of 350 cans of milk, one each to 500 people, with 52 cans left over.

There is another answer which is given for healing: 'explicable but not yet explained'. René Laurentin, just quoted, is a French theologian and journalist and has been involved in the commission at Lourdes, which is charged with the examination of reported miracles. He has described its procedure. It is ultimately up to the ecclesiastical authorities to authenticate a miracle, and they are so strict that none was authenticated from 1965 until 1977. At an earlier stage in the investigation however an international medical commission has to pass final judgment at the scientific level. It has to answer three questions:

1. Was there sickness – and of what kind?
2. Was there cure: complete, instantaneous?
3. Was the cure or healing inexplicable by science?

Laurentin says that the doctors have no problem with the first two questions. However it is the nature of science to deny the inexplicable, so they usually respond to the third question by adding the clause 'inexplicable – in the present state of science'. This confuses the issue because according to the juridical norms set out by Rome such a restriction voids the testimony of medicine:

> Rationalism in principle always has a way out. It always asks for something more. This is what struck me on the occasions when I took part in the verification process of miracles. There were always doctors who voted against verification, because they wanted one more test. And if they had gotten it, I think they would have asked for still another, without end. . . But the scientific evaluation does not touch the spiritual effects which a cure may have on the subject or those who witnessed the cure.

And in Case Records 2.2 and 2.3 we have seen a glimpse of these.

It is usually possible to assert that, although a fact may be inexplicable at the moment, the answer is just round the corner: next year, next decade, next century. Miracle is therefore rarely provable. At the end of the day much depends on our mind-set; what Swinburne[10] refers to as our *Weltanschauung* 'world-view'. We noted in Chapter 1 David Hume's rigid requirements for acceptance of a miracle, and asked if Case Record 1.1 would suit him. It would not have done so. He refers[11] to current cases in Paris of curing the sick, giving hearing to the deaf and sight to the blind, which 'were immediately proved on the spot, before judges of unquestionable integrity, attested by witnesses of credit and distinction, in a learned age, and on the most eminent theatre that is now in the world'. Nevertheless he refused point-blank to credit such testimony: 'And what have we to oppose to such a cloud

of witness but the absolute impossiblity or miraculous nature
of the events which they relate.'

People do not like miracles if it upsets their world-view.
The Parisian events Hume referred to concerned the healings,
immediately on his interment in 1727, at the grave of a
humble Jansenist deacon, François de Paris. A report
commissioned by the cardinal, which indicated that there
were indeed genuine healings, was suppressed. Jansenists
were out of favour and the authorities did not like the
miracles. In 1732 the cemetery was closed by royal decree
and devotions at the tomb prohibited. Colin Brown[12] records
that this act provoked the anonymous graffito: 'By order of
the king, God is forbidden to perform miracles in this place.'

An Overlooked Possibility

While we have been considering the wisdom, in fact the
necessity, of looking for simple medical explanations of apparently miraculous cures, there is a complementary possibility
to be borne in mind.

A consultant paediatrician writes to me:

> A few years ago I had a patient with measles encephalitis
> who made a rapid and complete recovery – one of those
> who experience complete spontaneous resolution. This
> might have been the end of the story had I not been asked,
> some eighteen months later, to speak at a Youth Fellowship
> meeting in a local church. After the meeting one of the
> teenagers approached me to ask if I remembered this child
> with encephalitis who was a relation of hers. In conver-
> sation with the youth leader and the vicar afterwards I
> mentioned this, and the good recovery the child had made.
> 'Yes,' replied the vicar, 'as soon as we heard your diagnosis
> we arranged an all-night prayer meeting in the church to
> pray for her recovery.'

The paediatrician concludes: 'I just wonder how many other

instances of "spontaneous resolution" are related to such united, believing, persevering, intercession?'
It is a point well worth pondering.

1. D. M. Lloyd-Jones, 'The supernatural in medicine', repr. in *The Doctor Himself and the Human Condition* (London, CMF 1982), p. 94.
2. K. M. Hay, 'Survival against the Odds', *British Medical Journal*, 291 (1985), pp. 1805–6.
3. T. C. Everson and W. H. Cole, 'Spontaneous regression of cancer: preliminary report', *Annals of Surgery*, 144 (1956), pp. 366–83.
4. D. W. Smithers, 'Spontaneous regression of tumours', *British Journal of Radiology*, 13 (1962), pp. 132–7.
5. 'Bede's Prose Life of St Cuthbert', II; and 'A Life of St Cuthbert by an anonymous monk of Lindisfarne', ch. 4; in *Two Lives of St Cuthbert*, ed. B. Colgrave. Cambridge University Press 1940. Bede's Life is also in *The Age of Bede*. London, Penguin 1983.
6. V. Edmunds and C. G. Scorer (eds), *Some Thoughts on Faith Healing*, 3rd rev. edn. London, CMF 1979.
7. C. Brown, *Miracles and the Critical Mind*. Exeter, Paternoster; and Grand Rapids, M. B. Eerdmans 1984.
8. *Daily Light on the Daily Path: readings for the mornings and evenings of the year*. London, n.d.
9. R. Laurentin, *Miracles in El Paso?* (Ann Arbor, Servant Books 1982), p. 49.
10. R. Swinburne, *The Concept of Miracle*. London, Macmillan 1970.
11. qu. in Swinburne, p. 16.
12. *Miracles and the Critical Mind*, p. 64.

3

The Church and Healing

What Do We Mean by Healing?

Recently I admitted a woman into one of my gynaecological beds for investigation of abdominal pain. As the symptoms were bizarre the houseman taking her history went into it in considerable detail. Suddenly the patient flared, 'I know what's wrong with me. Tell me how to get rid of my husband.' That anecdote reminds us that men and women are not just bodies, but body and mind. Medicine recognises that healing involves both.

Around the same time another woman came to my out-patients clinic following a termination of pregnancy three months earlier. She told me that although not a Roman Catholic she had been making her confession to an RC priest, over and over, twice a week, in an endeavour to salve her conscience. And that anecdote reminds us that men and women are not just body and mind, but body, mind and spirit. Very many therapeutic efforts are frustrated by the failure of doctors to realise this. But not all doctors are blind. J. S. Stewart,[1] that doyen of preachers, tells of 'an eminent psychiatrist who always sent his patients to hear so-and-so preach because, "He preaches the forgiveness of sins." ' And the patients of a local RC general practitioner are sent to our Scripture Union bookshop to buy Merlin Carothers' *Prison to Praise*,[2] with its plea for a revolutionary attitude of praise in all the vicissitudes of life.

Healing and health require that in these three compart-ments of our being we are whole. But even that is not the complete story. We do not live like lone castaways on a desert island. We are linked by a web of relationships to spouse, children, parents, colleagues and neighbours. When these relationships turn sour our health is affected. Those areas give us a big enough canvas. It would be possible to extend 'healing' to cover relationships between races and societies but such semantic liberties would devalue the word for our purpose and are therefore not to be considered in this work.

From a reading of the New Testament it is clear that our Lord and his followers dealt with all three parts of men and women and intended the Church to follow suit. Paul's wish for the Christians in Thessalonica was, 'may you be kept sound in spirit, mind and body, blameless until the coming of our Lord Jesus Christ' (1 Thess. 5:23 JBP). When eventually we enter into our inheritance, not just forgiven but unblemished, not just healed but whole, then we will enjoy total health – but not until then. Meanwhile Christians find that although all three aspects of our being are renewed, for each part that renewal is different in duration.

As far as our spirit is concerned, as soon as we come back to our loving waiting Father and accept forgiveness we receive everlasting life, a new quality of life that is 'for keeps', for this life and the next uninterruptedly.

The new Christian's whole mind-set has to alter in obedience to the instruction: 'Adapt yourselves no longer to the pattern of this present world, but let your minds be remade and your whole nature thus transformed' (Rom. 12:2 NEB). But even so our minds are still subject to human limitations and constrained by ageing. Unlike our spirits, therefore, they will need a quantum leap on reaching heaven.

But as far as our bodies are concerned it is a different matter again. Some Christians after a hundred healthy years will 'fall asleep', while others deformed by congenital disease and scarred by multiple surgical onslaughts may give up in childhood. No matter, each of us on reaching heaven will receive a new body, recognisably ours but very different – for few of our present functions will be needed there. We do not envisage having to combat heavenly infections, nor frequent celestial loos. As Paul put it to the Christians in Philippi, 'We are citizens of heaven, and we eagerly wait for our Saviour to come from heaven, the Lord Jesus Christ. He will change our weak mortal bodies, and make them like his own glorious body' (3:20–1 GNB).

Physical healing in this life must therefore be purely temporary, necessarily so as it concerns our terrestrial bodies. Lazarus, raised from the dead by Jesus, would one day die again and be carried back to his tomb. Physical healing, being temporary, is therefore unimportant in the eternal welfare of anybody, and this is as true of miraculous healing as of medical. When God does heal a person miraculously it is not a stage in his or her eternal perfection achieved ahead of the rest of us. That, for every one of us, has to wait. We are still caterpillars, we are not yet butterflies.

It may well be asked, then what is the purpose of a healing miracle? Why does God bother? Surely because miracle is a sign, and of the various words for 'miracle' in the Greek New Testament (for which Archbishop Trench's study should be consulted)[3] this is one of the two most frequently used, and especially favoured by John. We shall see in Chapter 6 that it was a sign of the coming of the kingdom. And not just an external attesting sign but an integral part of the salvation announced, reaching beyond the merely spiritual to the psychological and physical.

As ours is a holistic salvation our Lord's miracles included healing of the body. But being a sign, not a programme, it was selective, specific, individual. This was a point precociously made by nine-year-old Martyn Lloyd-Jones.[4] His minister catechising the Sunday School class asked, 'Why did Jesus say, "Lazarus, come forth"?' Martyn's reply was, 'In case they all came forth.'

Jesus demonstrated this holistic healing during his earthly ministry, but what happened after his ascension? Was it back to the bad old days? We can perhaps get a hint of the issue from an episode in the Second World War. In 1942 a force of Canadian and other Allied troops landed at Dieppe. For a brief glorious moment the French must have seen it as the dawn of liberation. In a few hours however the surviving troops withdrew across the Channel, and the inhabitants of Dieppe were left again to the mercies of their oppressors. Is that what was meant to happen to the believers after the ascension? The kingdom had been announced by Jesus: 'The Spirit of the Lord has been given to me, for he has anointed me. He has sent me to bring the good news to the poor, to proclaim liberty to captives and to the blind new sight, to set the downtrodden free, to proclaim the Lord's year of favour' (Luke 4:18–19 JB). Was that proclamation later revoked? If not, then we would expect the signs and first-fruits of the kingdom to go on. That they did continue is illustrated in Chapters 4 and 7.

To fulfil their function as signs miraculous healings, inevitably temporary, need not be total. This is exemplified in the following history from the Royal Liverpool Hospital.[5]

CASE RECORD 3.1

In 1983 a man in his fifties presented with a bladder cancer. Recurrent bleeding had failed to respond to radiotherapy and he was referred from another hospital insisting on a second opinion. In the previous nine months he had had many cystoscopies/diathermies and had been transfused a total of 50 units of blood. He still continued to bleed. After assessment showed a poorly differentiated carcinoma (stage P3) invading the prostate and encircling the bladder neck, he was offered cystectomy (removal of the bladder). He refused and was treated by local surgery (transurethral resection) and a course of methotrexate (a cyto-toxic drug). Not surprisingly the therapeutic response was poor, and after counselling he was sent home for re-admission three weeks later for major surgery.

He was re-admitted with gross anaemia (Hb 7g/dl) and prepared for surgery. I arrived from holiday to find everything ready for cystectomy on my Monday morning operating list. I was told that the patient wished to see me urgently, and there was a letter from his wife which I was meant to read before operating. It read, 'We do not know what your beliefs are, but in the past fortnight we have become Christians... We have been to a healing service and are convinced that the prayer for cancer to be cleared will be answered... We beg you to perform another cysto-scopy before you attempt major surgery.'

I visited him and told him of my personal faith, and said I would only remove the bladder if it was badly diseased. At cystoscopy no tumour was present. There was old blood clot in the bladder but no trace of tumour. Marked changes from radiotherapy were present. The growth seen on the past three occasions by various members of the team had gone. My registrar confirmed that no tumour was now visible.

(Because of the bleeding and the irradiation-changes radical cysto-prostato-urethrectomy with pelvic mode dissection was performed and the urine diverted into an ileal conduit.) Histologically no tumour was found in the bladder, urethra or prostate and the nodes were clear. All earlier histology had shown invasive carcinoma. He is managing well. He and his wife appear to be growing in their faith and commitment.

The urologist whose account I quote verbatim has explained to me that the operation was still necessary despite the disappearance of the cancer, because the bladder had shrunk so much as to be no longer functional. In other words the life-threatening cancer had been miraculously cured, but not the complications. His account of that case concluded with the significant point that the greater healing was the bringing of this couple to everlasting life. This emphasises the point I made earlier that while physical healing can only be temporary, spiritual healing is eternal.

Medicine as Compassion

While throughout history healing of the spirit has been recog-nised as the responsibility of the Church, increasingly healing of the body has become the province of medicine.

But we must notice in passing that there have been Christians who in their hurry to get to heaven have had no interest in healing. Bede[6] records the passing of the Abbess of Barking in these words: 'Aethelburh, beloved of God, was taken from the prison-house of the flesh.' That was written in the eighth century. However only ninety years ago in her autobiography, Thérèse of Lisieux[7] implied that she certainly would not have sought healing:

I had never felt so strong, and this strength lasted me out till Easter. But on Good Friday Jesus had a present for me; nothing less that the hope of seeing Him quite soon in heaven. What a wonderful day to look back on. . . I had scarcely laid my head on the pillow when I became conscious of what seemed like a warm tide that rose up, up, till it reached my lips. I wasn't sure what it was, but my soul was flooded with joy at the thought that I was going to die; surely I must be spitting blood? Only the lamp was out, so I had to wait till morning to make certain it was all right. It wasn't a long wait; my first thought on waking was of good news coming to me, and as soon as I got to the window I realised that there was no mistake. With an intense feeling of happiness, I cherished the conviction that Jesus, on the anniversary of His own death, was sending me His first summons.

She had understood that her profession at the age of seventeen was her wedding ceremony; now, aged twenty-four, she went forth to meet her Bridegroom.

That attitude on the part of some of its members has not prevented the Church co-operating in the work of healing. In view of the example and instruction of our Lord this was inevitable and right. In fact in the early centuries it was the principal, often almost the only source of succour for the sick. Each religious house had its infirmary: so in British medicine our charge-nurses to this day are called sister. As we use that title many times a day we are acknowledging the roots of our practice in the Church of the early Middle Ages. But it was then largely nursing; for cure they had to turn to the shrines.

47

However as time passes the Church has, by and large, left physical healing to the medical profession, and this is especially true of the churches of the Reformation. An apparent exception is the care by Christians of incurables, but that was a ministry of mercy, healing being considered out of the question.

The Victorians' benevolence and Christian concern also had a part to play. At the beginning of the nineteenth century their grandparents, influenced by the evangelical awakening, had worked for the emancipation of the slaves: now it was their turn to become aware of the terrible condition of the slums in the homeland. At mid-century the Cowgate dispensary 'for the indigent Irish poor' was started in Edinburgh, and some decades later William Booth, the founder of the Salvation Army, published a seminal plan for dealing with some of these problems. *In Darkest England and the Way Out*[8] runs to 300 pages including three on medical care:

> I have been thinking that if a little Van, drawn by a pony, could be fitted up with what is ordinarily required by the sick and dying, and trot round amongst the abodes of desolation, with a couple of nurses trained for the business, it might be of immense service, without being very costly. They could have a few simple instruments, so as to draw a tooth or lance an abscess, and what was absolutely requisite for simple surgical operations. . .

A realisation that the dominical command, 'Heal the sick', is still of some relevance today for the Church, is seen especially at times of spiritual renewal; but it is usually seen as involvement in orthodox medicine. From the twelfth century onwards the evangelical Waldensian brothers, on their lengthy secret journeys, practised medicine.[9] In 1746 John Wesley founded the first really free medical dispensary in England. His diary for 4 December records:

> I mentioned to the society my desiring of giving physic to the poor. About thirty came next day, and in three weeks about three hundred. This we continued for several years

till the number of patients, still increasing, the expense was greater than we could bear: meantime, through the blessing of God, many who had been ill for months or years were restored to perfect health.

The next year he published *Primitive Physic (an easy and natural method of curing most diseases).*[10]

However it was through the foreign missionary enterprise that the Church became deeply involved in medical work. Initially missionary work was evangelistic pure and simple, even although some of the earliest missionaries were medically trained. When I sat my first professional examination in the hall of the Royal Faculty of Physicians and Surgeons of Glasgow I found it comforting to have the portrait of David Livingstone looking down on me. But to his contemporaries he was seen as a missionary, not as a 'medical missionary'. In 1842 the Church Missionary Society informed a surgeon of its willingness to employ him as a catechist on the clear understanding that medicine was to be only an occasional occupation; while in 1861 the same society advised an applicant against medical training because 'it seldom served any useful purpose'.[11] Of course as time went on medical knowledge would be useful for the care of health of European missionaries, their dependants and local helpers. Lay missionary candidates were given rudimentary medical knowledge as part of their training before leaving home, and one such delivered my own mother (by forceps) of her first child.

However it was the discovery that some countries whose inhabitants were 'bigoted' could be opened up by medical work, which changed the whole picture, and colonial authorities were sometimes the prime movers in persuading missionaries to provide medical help. Whether working as missionaries or not, Christian doctors ever since have been in the forefront of introducing western medicine to the third world.[12]

Medicine: integral to the gospel

The foundation of the Edinburgh Medical Missionary Society in 1841 is pinpointed by C. P. Williams[13] as the beginning of a breakthrough. It saw medical work as imperative to fulfil our Lord's commission in all its breadth and fullness, and played its part by providing generations of missionary candidates with financial help for their medical course, with a hostel, and practical experience in evangelism and dispensary work in the Cowgate slums. (In a post-war flowering in the late 1940s it also, by serendipity, provided many of us with a like-minded, like-trained spouse.)

Medical missionary work having first been accepted for tactical pragmatic reasons – a means of winning men's hearts in preparation for winning their souls – was now seen to be an obligatory expression of divine compassion. In A. F. Walls's[14] phrase, the nineteenth-century medical missionary had become 'the heavy artillery of the missionary army'. But even although medical work was recognised to be an integral part of Christian missionary obedience, it was still the medicine of the schools. It was clear to those of us who were also ordained to the Christian ministry of word and sacraments that this was a different function from medical work.

The Church and Healing

Everything is now different. Christian bookshops have whole sections dedicated to the literature of healing; societies, journals and conferences abound. And their topic is not healing through medicine, but healing through the Church. We must now look for the causes of this new development.

Of prime importance, in my view, was the experience of missionaries. This worked in at least four ways:

1. Whereas in the home countries it was, and is, possible to live in a denominational ghetto, missionaries of various theological outlooks inevitably meet one another. Terence Ranger has recorded[15] the problems for Anglican missions in

central Africa in the face of competition both from Catholic missionaries bringing cults of Marian apparitions with their healing implications, and from American missionaries with their expectations of pentecostal healings.

2. Missionaries far distant from conventional medical care were often driven to the ultimate source of all help, God himself. My mother's diary records an incident in 1919 in the West Nile district of Uganda, three days' march from any doctor. She had developed food poisoning. My father, recovering from his third near-fatal attack of blackwater fever, crawled to her bedside. They thought she was dying, as so many of their colleagues had died. In desperation at her condition he took some oil in his hand and anointed her and prayed, claiming the promise recorded by James: 'Is any sick among you? Let him call for the elders of the church; and let them pray over him, anointing him with oil in the name of the Lord: And the prayer of faith shall save the sick, and the Lord shall raise him up' (5:14–15 av). She recovered. Such stories, reported at deputation meetings during furlough, must inevitably have made some people think.

3. Missionaries came face to face with witchcraft and demon-possession very similar to accounts in the gospel. The scornful attitude towards such ideas, which some of them brought up in liberal protestantism professed, proved difficult or impossible to sustain. My first real awareness that miraculous healings could occur nowadays came some forty years ago from a penny pamphlet by Dr Catherine Maddox, published by the China Inland Mission.[16] The story is so sharply focused as to be either true or a complete fabrication. The latter possibility is not acceptable to me. I had met Dr Maddox, and had unbounded admiration for the CIM whose mission-stations in West Szechwan had, for almost a year, been home to me after the retreat from Burma. Before Mao closed and bolted that door I was in fact on the list of potential candidates for missionary service in China, so I knew their standards of integrity. Although in the nature of the case supporting documents are not available I have no option but to believe this account, which I quote in Dr Maddox's words:

CASE RECORD 3.2

Satan, we read, 'smote Job with sore boils'. I believe it is a mistake to attribute all illness to the direct intervention of the devil. And yet Christ clearly suggests that some is his work, when He refers to a physically afflicted woman as one 'whom Satan hath bound'. I had a missionary patient with an abscess. I watched it developing and beginning to point as the pus formed. The abscess was delaying the patient's recovery from an operation, and God suddenly revealed to her and her husband that it was a direct enemy attack. Well, what was to be done in such a case? What I did was to come along with a local anaesthetic and a sharp knife! But I had been forestalled: the patient and her husband had resisted the enemy, and when I took the dressing off, there was no abscess there!

The question should have been unavoidable to the Christian world: if New Testament spiritual resources were available in that sort of medical case, might they not also be similarly available in ordinary pathological conditions? And if in the mission field, why not in the homelands?

4. Missionaries came into contact with peoples who had an integrated view of themselves, who saw sickness and healing as influenced by the spirit world. When such folk turned to Christ and were built into churches they naturally maintained this attitude and were baffled by the westerners' separation of physical problems from the spiritual. Taught to read, given the Scriptures in their own language, exhorted to believe them, they sometimes embarrassed missionaries by taking New Testament promises at face value, and finding them true.

In Britain interest in healing was stimulated also from a different direction, the revival of incarnation theology associated with the High Church movement. As Christ had dignified human flesh by being born into it, was the Church right to consider it of little importance? The Guild of Health was formed in 1904 to encourage co-operation with the medical profession in the practice of healing. It continues its work to this day. Bishop Maddocks[17] has summarised its aims as being to help people to experience within the fellowship of God's family the freedom and life promised by Jesus Christ, implementing this aim through prayer, sacrament and counselling, and attempting to heal the polarisation between the caring professions. It seeks to enable all members to study the interaction between physical, mental and emotional facts in well-being, and their relationship with the spiritual life in prayer and meditation.

However in 1905 something more challenging happened when James Hickson, an Anglican layman with experience of miraculous healings, started an organisation now known as the Divine Healing Mission.[18] Many people were healed in the next quarter of a century in the missions he held, almost always with episcopal blessing, in various parts of the world. It was his experience in particular which ensured that the subject of healing could no longer be ignored, and it was debated at the 1908 Lambeth Conference.

There was opposition from both wings! On the liberal side it was exemplified by Hensley Henson (Bishop of Durham 1920–39), who lamented,[19] 'The bishops want to be deceived', by what he termed the spiritual healing craze, and which was, he suspected, only a British version of 'the same movement of intellectual regression which in America is known as Fundamentalism'. (How wrong can you be? He did not know that even by the late 1980s many fundamentalists would not be reconciled to healing by the Spirit.) As for miraculous healing, it 'should be left in the hands of anthropologists and students of religion . . . it is not a Christian phenomenon. It has for Christians no religious significance'. He went on to quote with approval the words, written in 1910, of a famous doctor, Sir Clifford Allbut:

A careful study of all reported cures of this miraculous or miraculoid kind proves to the expert observers of today that they all – palsies, convulsions, and the rest, often inveterate cases – are and have been cures of one disease, and one only, hysteria . . . miraculous cures, so far as they are genuine, are cures by suggestion.

From the opposite wing the *English Churchman*, an evangelical journal, suspected that spiritual healing was being used for the purpose of imposing sacramental error upon the Church of England.

'The Ministry of Healing'

Since then the story as far as the English religious establishment is concerned has been long, tortuous and relatively uninspiring. Commissions have been appointed, on occasion involving the British Medical Association, and their Reports have eventually been published.

But while these committees and groups were meeting, God was still quietly active in healing. In Chapter 5 we will look at the experiences of Smith Wigglesworth, starting in the 1870s; and these were not unique in pentecostal circles in the first quarter of the twentieth century. Such, however, are the social and denominational battlements that they probably went unnoticed. In Scotland Cameron Peddie, a parish minister in the slums of Glasgow, witnessed the healing of members of his family at the hands of a medium. 'I was aflame with jealousy for the honour of my Lord . . . here was work which the Ministry of the Church should be doing in the name of Jesus Christ.' For five years he prepared himself spiritually and waited, until one morning in 1947, while peeling potatoes by the kitchen sink, God commissioned him: 'Joy filled my heart and overflowed in tears, helplessly I cried, like a child, the tears pouring from my eyes. All I could say was "Father, oh Father." ' What followed is recorded in *The Forgotten Talent: God's ministry of healing*.[20]

The reference in Case Record 3.2 to satanic powers, and in the last paragraph to mediums, raises the whole question of demonic powers, and of non-Christian healing. With memories of the witchhunts of a few centuries ago I am chary of mentioning such subjects. There is no doubt that there are healers who make no Christian profession, and healings in other religions, some of which we may accept as being ultimately from God. But there are also healings of much more sinister origin. Augustine declared that miracles may emanate 'either from seducing spirits or from God Himself', a point also made by Calvin: 'Satan perverts the things which otherwise would be works of God and misemploys miracles to obscure God's glory.' I am not so naive as to disbelieve in evil spirits, and the appointment of an official Anglican commission under the Bishop of Exeter to investigate exorcism demonstrates that I am not alone. However, mercifully my experience in this field is minimal and I do not propose to discuss this large subject further, except to counsel against the opposite mistake of seeing demons (I have even noted 'the spirit of abortion' personified) [21] in every sickness or problem.

However to return to the Anglican scene we must briefly look at a commission appointed by the archbishops in 1953, with a brief:

> to consider the theological, medical, psychological and pastoral aspects of Divine healing with a view to providing
> . . . a report designed to guide the Church to clearer understanding of the subject; and in particular to help the clergy in the exercise of the ministry of healing, and to encourage increasing understanding and co-operation between them and the medical profession.

The five bishops, seven other clergy and six doctors immediately ran into problems defining what they were talking about.

'Faith healing' was unsatisfactory. It was 'far from precise and may imply that a pre-requisite for healing is belief in the healer's powers; or belief that the sufferer will in fact recover; or belief that God wills recovery from a particular ailment.' 'Spiritual healing' was ambiguous, being used by those who claimed to be in touch with the 'spirit world', and also implying that other methods of healing were necessarily not spiritual. They found objection in their brief to the words, 'divine healing', in that they concealed that all healing comes from God. It could also imply that those with a healing gift 'who work outside the Church's life and fellowship have not received their gift from God'.

So they settled for:

> The Church's Ministry of Healing [which] is an integral part of the Church's total work by which men and women are to become true sons and daughters of God's kingdom. In it are to be employed all the means God has put at our disposal; the administration of the Word and Sacraments; the exercise of pastoral care; and the employment of all the many gifts of special kinds which God has given to individuals. Among the latter the skill and knowledge of those who have given themselves to the discipline of medical and nursing training are by no means the least.

The Report[22] runs to 84 pages but its kernel from our point of view lies in paragraph 53:

> This is not to deny for a moment the possible occurrence of extraordinary and medically inexplicable healings which present themselves to faith as miraculous. But the main strength of the testimony to the healing action of Christ in His body resides, not in occasional marvels, but in the numerous cases where, though nothing medically surprising is noted, faith sees God acting through the ministry of grace as well as through medical means.

It goes on to make recommendations solely in terms of the ministry of healing as an integral part of the clergy's activities, with the laying on of hands as a part of the services, especially Holy Communion.

At this distance, even to contemporaries, it does not seem an exciting new discovery of divine power. A similar Report to the General Assembly of the Church of Scotland, published the same year, and the World Council of Churches Report on the 1965 Tübingen Consultation,[23] were equally bland.

Local clergy/doctor groups, often top-heavy on the periphery of these disciplines, spring up and fade away. The perennial ethical discussions on abortion, euthanasia, and whatever happens to be the current topic of debate – *in-vitro* fertilisation, surrogate motherhood, and so on – stimulate interest for a while, but common ground for action on healing of specific individuals is usually sadly lacking. In 1956, in evidence to the Archbishops' Commission, the BMA[24] commented, 'From time to time during the last twenty years groups of doctors and clergy and interested laymen had met, but these groups appeared to dissolve without reaching any conclusion.' It has not changed.

'Homes of healing' have been brought into being, usually through the incredibly hard work and zeal of a dedicated individual. In England Burrswood in association with the name of Dorothy Kerin is an outstanding example.[25] A number have been short-lived. While serving on the committee of management of one of these homes I was acutely aware that none of us seemed clear about its purpose. It certainly provided a very comfortable caring environment for convalescence or retreat. The presence of chapel and chaplain and the availability of the sacraments could hardly fail to be beneficial. But how and what were we hoping to heal?

Although there was a High Church element in all this, especially through the Guild of St Raphael, it would probably be true to say that it was a broad Church Movement, both in the Anglican and Free churches. Evangelicals were rarely interested. I resigned from the Institute of Religion and Medicine when its membership was opened to any religion, for it was difficult to see how the work of the Third Person of the Trinity could be central. Doubtless I had misunderstood its *raison d'être*.

It is comforting to find that I am not alone in problems of this sort. Hugh Trowell is one of the most authoritative voices in the field. A senior physician, he was later ordained in the Anglican ministry, working full-time in hospital chaplaincies, and prepared some splendid study documents for the IRM. He has been very forthright:[26]

From the medical side, almost no Christian doctor or nurse has written a book of any weight in scholarship or in experience which sets forth how they can co-operate with those engaged in 'Christian Faith Healing' as that term has been traditionally used. . . One certainly must not believe that if one cures the spirit of man, whatever that means, that his bodily illness will improve or disappear. This sloppy thinking invades so much that is written about the Church's Ministry of Healing.

In 1969 he summed up his experience of some ten years as a parish priest and hospital chaplain during which he had not personally met anyone who had improved with respect to their physical condition after faith healing.

However almost all patients returned from a home of healing with improve morale, which could be a very important matter in facing prolonged disability.

The confusion is exemplified in the story of a blind official of the Guild of Health who was a help and an inspiration to many. Concerning his own blindness it is said that he maintained a simple outlook, combined with a radiant cheerfulness. 'I maintain that I have been healed, though my blindness has not been taken away, but I have been lifted above it, and it has become no handicap to me. I am healed.' In my own view, whatever the churchman may say, to the doctor this is a nonsense statement, an example of Orwellian 1984 newspeak. Trowell is no less blunt in his summing up of the whole scene:

> The Church has a ministry to the incurable, it can offer compassion, it can encourage cheerfulness, it can pray with them and for them. It can transmit grace. To call all this 'healing' to an ordinary Englishman is nearer to lying than to love. . . It must be stated categorically that the use of the term 'Ministry of Healing' is most misleading, if not definitely deceptive.

If Trowell is right why then the continuing torrent of books published under such a title? Why 'healing services', advertised in some cases by clergy who have never seen a physical disease cured? Let us face the question: has the whole enterprise been a mistake, a waste of time, energy and money? No, there have been some useful results. Great numbers of church workers and caring professionals have come to understand each other's problems. Training in counselling has been given. In role-plays we have obtained a glimpse of issues we did not realise existed. Psychosomatic illness, depression, inter-personal stresses, are now understood in a new way, and the relationship of these to bodily health is recognised. More important, some invalids have entered into a new understanding of God's care for their whole being, and have received inner peace.

But I detect in all these activities a wistful longing. Having woken up to the fact that the God who has good news for the spirit of men and women also cares for body and mind, we cannot avoid asking, does not the New Testament suggest and promise something better than we have yet seen? Surely the promise of Christ that his followers would do greater things than he had done meant something more than benevolence to the needy and imparting cheerfulness to the ill? It did, as the Holy Spirit was about to show us.

Healing Miracles of the Holy Spirit

In a paper read to the Ecclesiastical History Society in 1981[27] Stuart Mews clarifies the situation:

> We should be wary of assuming that the Lambeth Conference resolutions mark stages in the cumulative build-up of interest in spiritual healing; they should rather be seen as responses to waves of interest which have ebbed and flowed throughout this century. Much of the contemporary concern seems to be inspired directly (or sometimes indirectly) by the movement for charismatic renewal, and arises out of a fresh discovery in the 1960s of the possibility of this ministry, rather than from a direct continuation and enlargement of the experiments and enterprises of the 1920s and 1950s. . .

That fresh discovery was not of a ministry of the Church, but of the power of the living God. This power is demonstrated in our next case. One day in 1982 my post contained a circular letter from a missionary doctor in Pakistan. Tucked away in the middle of a long paragraph was the following story.

CASE RECORD 3.3

And here is Kamro who knows that Jesus has saved her. She had a profuse haemorrhage due to a clotting defect in the blood following a Caesarean Section last Sunday. This condition responds only to transfusions of triple- or quadruple-strength plasma and fancy drugs in England. Here, where these things are not available, it responds to the prayer of faith in Jesus' name, and I suppose the meagre two pints of blood donated by her brothers, one of whom is a professional footballer, helped to keep her strength up as her own blood poured alarmingly into the bed. Her premature baby daughter lying in the blue-painted cot at the foot of the bed is absolutely sweet and doing very well.

I stopped and read the paragraph again. As an obstetrician I have met this problem of coagulation failure on a few occasions. They are among the most desperate problems we face, sending us running to the telephone to seek the help of haematologist and blood transfusion service. In his standard textbook[28] Ian Donald quotes a case requiring a 21 pint transfusion; but even that is not an unusual figure.

This story from Pakistan is so startling that a number of questions occur to the medical reader. Is the diagnosis likely to be correct? Does the account emanate from some fringe religious group of suspect views? Is the story as reproduced for circulation in Britain accurate?

The letter was written by Dr Ruth Coggan, a specialist obstetrician and gynaecologist, who in the year of this incident was elevated to the fellowship of our college. There are no doubts as to the accuracy of the medical details. She is the daughter of a recent Archbishop of Canterbury, and a missionary of the Church Missionary Society; orthodoxy is therefore not in question. I wrote to her for fuller details which I reproduce verbatim:

Kamro, who had had 7 previous pregnancies, and was aged about 35, was first seen by me on 13 May 1982 at about 8 months gestation. (You will be amused at the vagueness of all these estimates.) She was complaining of bleeding on and off for five months, with intermittent abdominal pain. She was urged to come into hospital, but only did so on 15 May, after a very heavy loss the preceding night. On examination her blood pressure was markedly raised (170/110mmHg). She had marked oedema of feet and abdominal wall. She was anaemic (Hb.78%). Her uterus was 32 weeks size. The babe was lying correctly but the head was very high and poorly felt. She was admitted for supervised bed-rest and the blood pressure settled a little (to 160/100 mmHg) but on the day after admission she had another very heavy bleed. I accordingly performed lower segment Caesarean Section. Unfortunately I was completely unable to locate any cerebrospinal fluid to put in a spinal anaes-thetic as I usually do, so I did the operation under local infiltration (1% lignocaine) plus intravenous medication (pethedine 100 mgm altogether). A low transverse incision in the lower uterine segment of the uterus went right through the placenta which was found to be extremely adherent to the lower uterine flap and was raggedly removed. Copious dark blood clot was released on entering the uterus. A 2.3 kg female child was delivered, who thrived. (I'm afraid I have no note about the absence or presence of retroplacental blood clot, but the placenta was pretty chewed up by the time I had incised it and removed adherent bits.)

There was heavy blood loss at the time of operation and profuse blood loss post-operatively, not clotting. Deep pools of unclotted blood between the patient's thighs and pad – heavy and prolonged trickling. Oxytocin (a drug to make the uterus contract) was added to the dextrose-saline drip, and then we prayed with the patient after explaining to her about Jesus in whose name we had prayed for her before the operation, and who was a great healer. I also told her that we were not going to worry. I had seen Jesus heal this condition before and was sure He was going to heal her. We then arranged to get two pints of blood for her. Brisk bleeding continued. First clot was seen 48 hours after operation. Heavy blood loss had continued until that but her general condition gave no cause for concern after the initial post-operative examination at two hours. We prayed with her again on the night of the operation, and then to thank Jesus for healing when she went home with her baby on the tenth day. It is a privilege and thrill to be able to take part in the Lord's work of healing, and see Him at work.

We have satisfactorily settled the question whether the initial account received was accurate. And we have discovered that the woman's needs were more desperate than had been suggested in the circular letter. Kamro was anaemic and rapidly becoming more so. She was hypertensive (had high blood pressure.) She had bleeding from the placenta which would inevitably kill her if she were not delivered by Caesarean section, and in view of her two bleeds in two days this operation could not be postponed to allow her condition to improve. However we can ignore all the other problems of her condition, because what was going to kill Kamro very soon was the failure of her blood to clot. Blood coagulation is an extraordinarily complex matter involving a cascade of reactions the final stage of which is the conversion of a material normally present in the blood (fibrinogen) into blood clot. If, as in Kamro's case, all the fibrinogen has already been used there is nothing to form clot: the patient goes on bleeding until death. Massive volumes of fresh blood (to provide fibrinogen) and/or other extremely expensive substances containing clotting-factors, are mandatory if the patient is to be saved. These were not available. That she did not somehow produce enough fibrinogen or receive sufficient from her brothers' donations, is evidenced by the fact that the blood still failed to clot until forty-eight hours post-partum (by which time the normal recovery of fibrinogen production would have occurred).

It is not usually useful to ask what is the nature of a miracle, but that question can probably be answered in this case. Heavy loss continued for forty-eight hours after operation, 'but her general condition gave no cause for concern after the initial post-operative examination at two hours'. During those forty-eight hours we may estimate that Kamro lost at least her complete blood volume, possibly two or three times over. But despite this her condition did not deteriorate. She behaved as though God was replacing the blood as quickly as she was losing it.

I make no apology for going into clinical detail in reporting this case because its implications are enormous. None of the alternative explanations we have examined in Chapter 2 can be entertained here. If the story is true – and I have gone to pains to meet doubts in advance – then we do not need any other case to prove that God intervenes to heal miraculously in the 1980s.

Surprisingly, hard evidence of miraculous healing is not good news in some theological circles. Martyn Lloyd-Jones, some time first assistant to a famous physician, Lord Horder, in Harley Street and later minister of Westminster Chapel,[29] has identified three groups of people who reject the idea *in toto*. The first rejects it out of hand – the whole thing is bogus, impossible by definition; and the second because, nature being a closed system, miracles are impossible. He places his third group under the heading of 'biblical':

> those who pay little attention, if any, to all these claims because they hold dogmatically the view that the miraculous, and all such spiritual manifestations, ended with the apostles, and that, once we were given the completed canon of the New Testament, all such unusual phenomena came to an end.

This is an argument we will have to consider carefully in Chapter 7. In the same lecture Lloyd-Jones goes on to say:

> We must be careful that we do not fall into the same error into which the Roman Catholic Church fell in the case of Copernicus and Galileo. The leaders of that Church rejected the facts, you remember, because they did not fit into their theory. We must be very careful that we are not caught at the same point, and refuse to recognize facts because our theory regards them as impossible. Indeed I sometimes have a fear that our dogmatism in these matters is far too similar to that of the Communists and their treatment of Lysenko. We must not ban any findings on purely theoretical or doctrinaire grounds. We must have an open mind and be ready to accept facts and to examine them.

To sum up: it seems clear that we are not being asked to take on board some new facet of the Church's manifold activities. We stand in awe before a mighty God who, in this decade, is exercising his power in physical healing.

With this experience and knowledge a whole new area of co-operation between Spirit-filled doctors and Christians: congregations, fellowships, prayer-groups, is rapidly developing.[30] There are general practices which operate on church premises, and an increasing number of young doctors work only part-time in order to devote energies to the local fellowship and community. At last we are beginning to see something of true holistic medicine: body, mind and spirit all being renewed by God the Holy Spirit.

John Wyclif,[31] in the first extant English translation of the New Testament, for the Greek word *soteria*, which we normally translate 'salvation', rendered 'health'. So he has Paul telling the Roman Christians that he is not ashamed of the gospel because it is 'the virtue of health for believers'. Wyclif was obviously on to something: it has taken us a long time a catch up.

1. J. S. Stewart, *A Faith to Proclaim*. London, Hodder & Stoughton 1953.
2. M. Carothers, *Prison to Praise*. Plainsville, NJ, Logos; and London, Hodder & Stoughton 1972.
3. R. C. Trench, *Notes on the Miracles of our Lord* (London, Parker 1850), pp. 1–8.
4. I. H. Murray, *D. Martyn Lloyd-Jones: the first forty years* (Edinburgh, Banner of Truth 1984), p. 5.
5. R. Jameson, *In the Service of Medicine* (January 1984).
6. *Bede's Ecclesiastical History of the English People*, ed. B. Colgrave and R. A. B. Mynors (Oxford, Clarendon Press 1969), 4.IX. The standard work; there are many English translations.
7. Thérèse of Lisieux, *The Autobiography of a Saint*, tr. R. Knox. London, Harvill Press 1958.
8. W. Booth, *In Darkest England and the Way Out*. London, Salvation Army 1890.
9. P. Biller, '*Curate infirmos*: the medieval Waldensian practice of medicine', in *The Church and Healing*, ed. W. J. Shiels, *Studies in Church History*, vol. XIX. Oxford, Blackwell 1982.
10. John Wesley, diary 1746; and *Primitive Physic: an easy and natural method of curing most diseases*. London 1747; many later editions.
11. C. P. Williams, 'Healing and evangelism: the place of medicine in later Victorian Protestant missionary thinking', in *The Church and Healing*, ed. Shiels, pp. 271–84.
12. See *Heralds of Health*, ed. S. G. Browne. London, CMF 1986; and specialised local studies, e.g. R. Schram, *A History of the Nigerian Health Services*. Ibadan 1971.
13. Williams, p. 281.
14. A. F. Walls, 'The heavy artillery of the missionary army: the domestic importance of the nineteenth-century medical missionary', in *The Church and Healing*, ed. Shiels, p. 189.
15. T. Ranger, 'Medical science and Pentecost: the dilemma of Anglicanism in Africa', in *The Church and Healing*, ed. Shiels, pp. 333–66.
16. C. Maddox, *The Enemy*. London, China Inland Mission n.d. I would like to record my gratitude to officials of the Overseas Missionary Fellowship (successors of CIM) in England, America and Singapore, who searched for a copy; and to Dr Chris Maddox who eventually found one for me.
17. M. Maddocks, *The Christian Healing Ministry*. London, SPCK 1981.
18. S. Mews, 'The revival of spiritual healing in the Church of England 1920–26', in *The Church and Healing*, ed. Shiels, pp. 299–331.
19. H. H. Henson, *Notes on Spiritual Healing*. London, Williams & Norgate 1925.
20. J. C. Peddie, *The Forgotten Talent: God's ministry of healing*. London, Collins 1966; repr. Evesham, A. James-1985.

21. B. and S. Banks, *Ministering to Abortion's Aftermath* (Kirkwood, Mo., Impact Books 1982), p. 5.
22. *The Church's Ministry of Healing: Report of the Archbishops' Commission.* London, CIO 1958.
23. See *Spiritual Healing: Report to the General Assembly of the Church of Scotland.* 1958; and *The Healing Church: Report on the Tübingen Consultation 1964.* Geneva, World Council of Churches 1965.
24. *Divine Healing and Co-operation between Doctors and Clergy.* London, BMA 1956.
25. D. M. Arnold, *Dorothy Kerin: called by Christ to heal.* London, Hodder & Stoughton 1965.
26. H. Trowell, *Study Notes on Faith Healing, Secular and Religious Faith Healing, Fringe Medicine, Miracles of Healing.* London, Institute of Religion and Medicine 1969.
27. S. Mews, 'The revival of spiritual healing in the Church of England 1920–26', op. cit.
28. *Practical Obstetric Problems*, 5th edn. London, Lloyd-Luke 1979.
29. D. M. Lloyd-Jones, 'The supernatural in medicine', repr. in *The Doctor Himself and the Human Condition* (London, CMF 1982), pp. 81–98.
30. e.g. some are linked and encouraged by the organisation Caring Professions Concern.
31. Wyclif, qu. R. V. Spivey, 'Prayer and Healing', in *Religion and Medicine: essays by members of the Methodist Society for Medical and Pastoral Psychology*, ed. J. Crowlesmith (London, Epworth 1962), pp. 113–24.

4

Miracles:
a constant phenomenon?

Taking our working definition that miraculous healing is healing of a pathological condition of the body in a medically inexplicable way, in association with prayer to God: if this is happening today is it a new activity of God's or has it been present throughout the Church age? In this chapter let us look at the evidence. The theological arguments we will leave to Chapter 6.

It would be possible (though not in the time available to a practising gynaecologist) to produce a large volume of reputed miraculous healings. Taken merely at face value they would be of little use. As it is impracticable to obtain direct confirmatory evidence we will have to rely on the stature of the reporter, and his closeness in time to the events. For all my records I have gone back to contemporary sources. My eclectic choice falls on Martin in the fourth century; the Northumbrian saints of the Celtic tradition in the seventh century; and the first generation of the Scottish reformers in the sixteenth century. This gives us a wide spread, both in time and theological outlook.

Martin of Tours (c. 336–397)[1]

The leprosy settlement of Kumi lies deep in the bush, and is not unlike many others in East and West Africa. However we were surprised and intrigued to find that its mud-and-thatch church was dedicated to St Martin of Tours. Why should a twentieth-century group of Ugandan Christians have as their patron saint a monk-bishop who lived in fourth-century Gaul?

The choice was made by the patients, who no doubt identified themselves with the poor man destitute of clothing whose pleas for help were disregarded by other bystanders but who was befriended by Martin, then a young cavalryman in the Roman army. He divided his cloak in two, gave one half to the man and wrapped the remaining half round himself. That night he had a vision of Christ arrayed in the part of the cloak he had given to the beggar, and heard him announce to the multitude of angels, 'Martin, who is still a catechumen, clothed me in this robe.'

Leaving the army he became a monk, attracted disciples and acquired a reputation as a healer, a holy man whose prayers carried weight in the court of heaven. In her magisterial study, *St Martin and his Hagiographer*,[2] Clare Stancliffe points out that we can confirm the genuineness of his reputation as a healer from a story which has a completely different purpose. Martin's election as Bishop of Tours, despite his own reluctance, was achieved by a hoax, for the problem was how to winkle him out of his monastery. A townsman was sent to him with a sob-story about his wife being very ill, requesting Martin to come at once and heal her. When on this errand of mercy Martin came to Tours and the mob crowded round and insisted on his immediate consecration. Thereafter there was no question of his being called upon to demonstrate his powers, so the opportunity of boosting his healing reputation was neglected, obviously being unnecessary.

'The gift of accomplishing cures was so largely possessed by Martin that scarcely any sick persons came to him for assistance without being at once restored to health.' We are told of a paralysed girl who was moribund. Her father, clasping Martin's knees, said, 'I believe that through you she will be restored to health.' Martin retorted that this was a matter not in his own hands, that he was not worthy to be the instrument through whom the Lord should make display of his power. Nevertheless he felt constrained to go with the man. 'Betaking himself to his familiar arms in affairs of that kind, he cast himself down on the ground and prayed.' He then blessed oil and poured it into the mouth of the girl, who recovered. In addition to healings of paralysis, fever, menorrhagia, leprosy, poisoning, snake-bite and other un-specified conditions, three cases are recorded of Martin raising the dead – and one of these afterwards told that he had already reached the judgment throne.

Can we really be expected to believe any of this? I think so, for three reasons:

1. How else are we to explain Martin's influence, which even at the time was immense? In Britain the first Christian we can flesh-out is Ninian, 'amid whose prayers in his lonely rock-hewn cave by the Solway, the Church of Scotland came to birth', as Dr Duke finely puts it.[3] Tradition maintains that Ninian visited Martin at Tours. Whether or not this visit actually took place it remains that the first church in Scotland, the Candida Casa at Whithorn, was dedicated to Martin within a year or two of his death, as were a whole string of other churches shortly after.

2. The status of the contemporary record. While it is easy to assume that the Martinian stories are fairy-tales spun in an ignorant era, that would be to misjudge the age of the late Roman Empire. The Life was written during his lifetime by Sulpicius Severus who, after visiting Martin gave up his legal practice and adopted the ascetic life himself. It is obvious from this biographer's other writings, notably his History, that he adopted a scholarly critical approach to evidence, writing for the cultivated Roman intelligentsia who had not yet accepted the Christian faith. These people were nobody's fools. It was a world where intellectually we would feel at home; in the absence of tape-recorders the well-off paid short-hand writers to accompany them to Augustine's Bible studies. It was a world where travel was still relatively easy, and correspondence between scholars customary. There was constant coming and going between Rome, the forward imperial headquarters at Trier in the Rhineland, Augustine's Carthage, Jerome's Jerusalem, and Spain and Egypt.

Even at the time there were those who doubted the stories. A considerable contemporary literature still exists,[4] conveniently Englished for us by F. H. Hoare in *The Western Fathers*, which includes Sulpicius's further writings in the next decade. In these he responds to criticisms and doubts by quoting the names of witnesses, some of senatorial status, who were still available for questioning. A further proof of Sulpicius's veracity is that he includes material a less honest biographer would have omitted: that Martin remained a soldier for some time after his baptism; this – by the time the book was written – would have debarred him from the priesthood; that Martin, who went home to convert his parents, was successful only with his mother; that when trapped by fire in his room his initial reaction was to panic and he was burnt, before realising he should turn to prayer. Such inconvenient facts would not have found their way into a fictional or idealised account.

3. It rings a bell in our own experience. There is a contemporary echo in Clare Stancliffe's discussion as to why some of his acquaintances did not like Sulpicius's biography: his emphasis on Martin's gifts of healing may have made some Christians uneasy:

> Christianity having spread throughout the empire such miracles were no longer needed... For churchmen who belonged to this traditional school of thought the fourth century upsurge in the cult of martyrs and its accompanying miracles was perhaps as disturbing as is the charismatic movement for many traditionally-minded Christians today.

Sulpicius's aim is not primarily to show Martin the miracle worker, but Martin the man endowed with *virtus* spiritual power. This was not an attribute of his episcopal rank, for more than once he bemoaned the fact that he had had more power while a simple monk than after he became a bishop. Nor do I think it was solely an attribute of his ascetic life as a monk, for we find him, while still a soldier, described as 'a man full of God'. In turning to the documents written 1500 years ago it is Martin's spirit-filled character that is recognised immediately, despite the intervening centuries.

Martin, returning to his monastery after three days absence, found that life had departed from a catechumen . . . so hurries up to the mourning brethren who were saying the last offices, with tears and lamentations. *But then laying hold, as it were, of the Holy Spirit, with the whole powers of his mind,* Martin orders the others to quit the cell in which the body was lying; and bolting the door, he stretches himself at full length on the dead limbs of the departed brother. Having given himself for some time to earnest prayer, *and perceiving by means of the Spirit of God that power was present* he then rose up for a while, and gazing on the countenance of the deceased he *waited without misgiving for the result of his prayer and of the mercy of the Lord.* (my italics)

The lad revived.

In his life there are other evidences of the gifts of the Spirit, which although disbelieved by many scholars are true to the experience of the renewed church in the late twentieth century. Despite the fact that power over nature is not commonly reported today, many of Martin's experiences can be matched. Two contemporary parallels are worth relating.

1. It is recorded that in answer to Martin's prayer the volume of oil in a flask increased. This is usually poohpoohed, but not by those who have read, in *The Hiding Place*[5] the story of Corrie and Betsie ten Boom's experiences in Ravensbruck concentration camp in 1944. Betsie was ill, and Corrie tried to boost her health by putting on her slice of bread a drop of vitamin-concentrate from a tiny opaque bottle they had managed to smuggle in. But Betsie insisted on sharing the vitamins with others who were ill: more and more drops were given until twenty-five of their roommates were receiving them daily. Still the oil came. They encouraged themselves with Elijah's story of the bottle of oil which did not fail for the widow of Zarephath (1 Kings 17:11–16). The day a new supply of vitamins arrived they up-ended their bottle and found it empty.

71

2. Likewise the globe of fire once seen over Martin's head has baffled scholars. In northern Nigeria during the 'Gindiri Revival' of 1972 a pastor was knocked up to go to a church some distance away where the congregation had gathered after midnight, unbidden, to hear the word of the Lord. As he walked through the African bush that night he was guided by a globe of light, waist-high, going before him.

Martin had the gift of discernment of spirits, unmasking the devil when he appeared, once when posing as Christ. He also demonstrated the gift of knowledge, for instance his immediate awareness of the decisions of a synod held far away. We shall see evidence of this gift in present-day Co. Durham, in Case Record 6.2 (p. 126).

Martin, whatever he was doing, 'never slacked from prayer'. In his own lifetime he was recognised to be 'endowed with power', to be 'full of authority and grace'. When he died 'the world felt the departure of a believing man'. These are the words of his contemporaries. No one better demonstrates that the apostolic gifts, notably that of healing, still continued.

The Northumbrian Saints

Of the earlier part of the fourth century Bishop Maddocks[6] wrote:

> God raised up some of the greatest minds in history to serve him in this period . . . but after this golden age it was only individuals, men and women of the Spirit, who kept the flickering flame of the Church's commission and power to heal alight. Such were the desert Fathers, Martin of Tours, some of our own apostles of the north of England, and Francis of Assisi.

Don Bridge (*Signs and Wonders Today*)[7] has four pages on Bede and his contemporaries, so I feel vindicated in drawing attention to the Northumbrian saints. Nowhere is the dictum, 'History is the propaganda of the victors', better demonstrated than in the widespread belief that England was evangelised by Augustine and his colleagues from Canterbury. In the heptarchy this is true only of Kent. Almost all the rest of Anglo-Saxon paganism from the Firth of Forth to Wessex yielded to Christ as the result of one flaming generation of Celtic missionaries based on the island of Lindisfarne.[8] The records,[9] largely written by historians of the Roman obedience who had therefore no axe to grind, reveal a freshness, a zeal for our Lord, an uncluttered self-abandoning approach, a winsomeness, which have all the aroma of truth.

For miracles the greatest name is Cuthbert.[10] While we need not take seriously the recent claim that it was his provision of a thick mist which saved his cathedral of Durham from the Luftwaffe, the fact that such an event could be connected to a Northumbrian hermit who was bishop for a mere two years and died 1300 years ago, surely says something about his stature. He would leave his monastery on preaching tours, and 'would linger among the hill folk, calling the peasants to heavenly things both by the words he said, and by his virtuous deeds'. After years of quiet meditation on the Farne Islands, only when King Egfrith himself came to his hut to plead did he yield to the call to become a bishop. As bishop 'he was before all things fired with divine love, sober-minded and patient, diligent and urgent in devotion and prayer . . . always intent on heavenly things'. His prose biography by Bede names numerous eye-witnesses of Cuthbert's miracles, at least five of whom were still alive and in the Lindisfarne community, which had listened to, and approved as accurate, their accounts.

Bede[11] cites Aethilwald, one of Cuthbert's company, later abbot of Melrose, as eye-witness in the case which occurred when Cuthbert was making one of his usual preaching tours and had come to a village where there were a few nuns. One of these, a relation of Aethilwald's, was seriously ill, seized with pains in the head and all down one side, so that the doctors had given her up. Cuthbert's companions pointed this out to him and begged him to heal her. Full of pity for her wretchedness he anointed her with holy oil. She began to improve from that very moment, and in a few days completely recovered.

I record that story of life-threatening one-sided pain, the inability of medical skill to help, the anointing with oil, and the cure (although there are many much more spectacular miracles attributed to Cuthbert), because it parallels the following story recounted to me by the doctor involved.

CASE RECORD 4.1

In 1976 a group of four Christians, three expatriate missionaries and a national carpenter, travelled to a remote part of Nepal to start a leprosy clinic. While erecting a chimney stack the missionary builder fell on to a metal pipe on the upper veranda, and then rolled off and fell ten feet on to a concrete parapet. The missionary doctor was with him. The patient had obviously hurt his left side and at first was thought to have fractured his ribs. His blood pressure fell, his pulse rose, his abdomen became rigid and silent, and it became obvious that he was suffering from intra-abdominal haemorrhage due to a ruptured spleen.

The party had just arrived, the medical supplies as yet unpacked did not in any case contain surgical equipment. The doctor was only able to give him morphine and to set up a saline intra-venous infusion. They sent a police message for help which never got through. There were no human resources left.

After two hours the patient asked for prayer and anointing with oil. The three other Christians gathered round him. They read the biblical injunction from James 5:14–15. Cooking oil was used for anointing. His pulse and blood pressure rapidly improved. 'We believe', said my friend, 'that the Lord stopped the haemorrhage in response to prayer. We were alone in that situation for eight days. This time enabled us to integrate into that remote local community, and the people saw for themselves the effects of our prayers.'

As I have no choice but to accept the Nepalese story, I can

see no reason to doubt Bede's account, especially in view
of his reputation for scholarship: 'A careful and scrupulous
historian' is the verdict of Bertram Colgrave, his twentieth-
century editor.

Wilfrid, because of his later ecclesiastical policies, is not
everyone's favourite seventh-century saint, but in his personal
life he was simple and devout, as befitted someone who had
spent his teenage years in the Lindisfarne community.[12] As
Bishop of Hexham he built there the greatest church north
of the Alps. During its building the following incident
happened, as recorded by his assistant and biographer,
Eddius Stephanus:[13]

> One of the masons fell from a great height, broke his arms
> and legs, and dislocated his joints. He lay gasping his last.
> Wilfrid had been praying and weeping but now hastily
> summoned all the workmen. 'Let us show how great our
> faith is by praying together with one accord that God may
> send back the soul into this lad's body and hear our prayers
> for his life, even as he heard the prayers of St Paul.' They
> knelt and prayed that he who mocks at every good thing
> might have no victory to gloat over in this building. The
> bishop prayed after the manner of Elijah and Elisha and
> gave his blessing. The breath of life returned to the boy.
> The doctors bound up his arms and legs and he improved
> steadily day by day. He is still alive to give thanks to God
> and his name is Bothelm.

There are five facets to this story: the building of God's
house, the workman's fall resulting in skeletal injuries, the
sense that God's honour was at stake, communal prayer, and
cure. Those same factors are present in the case recorded by
Mother Basilea Schlink of the Evangelical Sisters of Mary, a
Lutheran order in West Germany, in *Realities: the miracles of
God experienced today*.[14] She describes the building of their
mother house and chapel, by the sisters themselves, shortly
after the Second World War.

CASE RECORD 4.2

We ventured out, trusting in God alone, and for His glory. According to our inner guidance we had not taken out accident insurance, or any other kind of insurance. Would God now permit some accident or mishap?

A sister fell on a freshly cemented floor on the second storey. She broke through, and to make it worse fell right on the edge of a piece of lumber. She was taken to hospital where the x-ray film showed a compound fracture of the pelvis.

This brought us very low before God. After a night of prayer – fraught with the worst temptations – I struggled through to a clear conviction: this accident had not been given in order to test us through a long time of suffering, rather it would serve to glorify God through a healing. It was then a matter of obedience to God's command. We did it, nevertheless, with trembling hearts. It was a great responsibility, the fearful question hung over our heads: what if she should become a cripple for the rest of her life? According to medical advice she should have remained in traction for many weeks. We were taking her home after two days. I had to sign for her release, accepting full responsibility. The doctor in charge spoke very earnestly to me, 'Mental sickness may perhaps be healed by prayer, but prayer will never mend a broken bone,' he warned me strongly.

At home Mother Martyria and I laid our hands on the sister and prayed. Some of the other sisters stood by and praised the victorious name of Jesus. The sister stood up from her bed. She had not been able to move on her bed without excruciating pain, and now she could actually stand on her feet. We looked at her, and for some moments could hardly take our eyes from her. Then we bowed in wonder and adoration before God – a God who indeed works miracles. Within two weeks the sister was completely healed, and presented herself to the doctor. The story spread through the country like wildfire. It magnified God's

glory far more than if He had protected us from danger
and accidents the whole time.

In response to enquiry I received a written reply from
Germany with the words: 'To the glory of God we can confirm
these events as eye-witnesses.' Further enquiry elicited the
reply that the sister afterwards walked without a limp.

If we accept Mother Basilea's account, and again we have
no other option, for it was widely published soon after the
event and the number of people able to contradict any exag-
geration must be legion; then there is no good reason for
doubting Eddius's account from Hexham, likewise published
during the lifetime of the man concerned. Throughout a long
stormy life Wilfrid was the centre of controversy, but to the
best of my knowledge this miracle was never called into
question.

The instigator of the Celtic mission was Oswald,[15] son of
the pagan king of Northumbria. While a refugee in Iona he
was converted by the successors of Columba, so when after
sixteen years in exile he attempted to gain his throne against
formidable odds he got his soldiers to make a great wooden
cross which he set up on the night before the crucial battle.
He obtained their promise to become Christians if they were
victorious, which they were; then he sent for a missionary
from Iona, and when Aidan came the king acted personally
as his interpreter, translating the gospel message from Celtic
into Northumbrian.

Many incidents demonstrating King Oswald's humility,
generosity, self-sacrifice and missionary zeal are recorded by
Bede. One story preserved elsewhere[16] tells that in a time of
dreadful pestilence with huge mortality the king entreated
God to take him and his family and spare his people. However
it is one of Bede's throw-away phrases that I find most significant: 'Because of Oswald's frequent habit of prayer and
thanksgiving he was always accustomed wherever he sat to
place his hands on his knees with the palms turned upwards.'
Whereas some modern secular historians use this as evidence
of his residual paganism – possibly associated with sacred

fertility rituals – it is a prayer posture many have rediscovered in recent days. In 1983 Richard Foster wrote in *Meditative Prayer*:[17] 'the hands outstretched or placed on the knees palm up gently nudge the inner mind into a stance of receptivity'. *Rex Deo delectus.* Bishop Lightfoot was surely right in applying to King Oswald the words originally written of King Josiah: 'like unto him was there no king before him, that turned to the Lord with all his heart, and with all his soul, and with all his might' (2 Kings 23:25 AV). There are no records of healings associated with Oswald during his life. Killed in battle, his body dismembered and hung up, it was daringly rescued by his brother and taken home for burial. Quite unexpectedly, unlooked for, the site of his death became a place of healing. Slivers of the cross he had raised at Heavenfield on the eve of his first victory were also found to have healing properties. As Peter Clemoes[18] puts it, Oswald's relics 'had given heaven and earth a lasting meeting-place of a special sort'. They were swiftly carried throughout Europe, and in our time some are still treasured in Tyrolean villages.[19]

Relics and Healing

What are we to make of this? Healings associated with relics do not figure in our thinking, and with God at our elbow I do not see why they should. The picture of the high Middle Ages when, to many, Christianity *was* relics and pilgrimages; when relics were stolen, hijacked, or faked, is not an edifying one. Despite the fact that in the pages of Ronald Finucane's detailed study, *Miracles and Pilgrims*,[20] we read evidence of some genuine cures, and of the care taken by some authorities to prevent fraud, our inclination is to spurn the subject.

Not surprisingly the reformers made a clean sweep. Knox's *Book of Discipline* lays down that idolatry was to be utterly suppressed including the adoration and retaining of images. The Anglican Thirty-Nine Articles was more specific. 'The worshipping as well of images as of reliques and also the invocation of saints is a fond thing vainly invented, and grounded on no warranty of Scripture, but rather repugnant to the Word of God.' In the State Papers of Henry VIII[21] we read that the king caused certain images and relics to be burnt and the more doubtful sort hidden away, 'following the example of King Hezekiah who destroyed the brazen serpent' (2 Kings 18:4).

With such admirable examples to guide us why deal with the subject of healing associated with relics at all? There is biblical precedent for it (I had almost added 'unfortunately'). 'Once while some Israelites were burying a man, suddenly they saw a band of raiders; so they threw the man's body into Elisha's tomb. When the body touched Elisha's bones, the man came to life and stood up on his feet' (2 Kings 13:21 NIV). So those of us who take a high view of scriptural inspiration have got a problem; which is not helped by the New Testament: 'through Paul God worked singular miracles: when handkerchiefs and scarves which had been in contact with his skin were carried to the sick, they were rid of their diseases and the evil spirits came out of them' (Acts 19:11–12 NEB). (Today there is a church in Oxford which, on the strength of that passage, posts 'prayer cloths' to the sick, and has obliged me with copies of letters from patients who report having physically benefited.)

As we are attempting to cover the field, let us try to get inside the minds of those Christians of earlier centuries, who were as dear to God as we are. This involves retracing our steps to the world of Martin. In his study, *The Cult of the Saints*,[22] Peter Brown talks of the geyser-like force with which belief in miracles of healing at tombs, or in connection with the relics of the martyrs, burst throughout the Mediterranean world in the late fourth century. Unfortunately it is all too easy to assume that in those days the average believer was – in Brown's splendid simile – 'like Winnie-the-Pooh "a bear of very little brain" '. Far from it, among them were some of the best brains the Church has ever had: Augustine of Hippo for a start. So let us try to understand them.

The inscription on Martin's tomb in Tours read: 'Here lies Martin the bishop, of holy memory, whose soul is in the hand of God; but he is fully here, present and made plain by miracles of every kind.' The human remains of a saint were understood to be still heavy with the fullness of the beloved person, who was at the same time intimate with God. Therefore the saint's tomb was a unique spot where earth and heaven made contact: almost an electric arc. And it was not merely a spatial contact, there was more to it than that. Victricius of Rouen, friend of Martin, a bishop on the very edge of the Roman world, wrote, 'Here are bodies where every fragment is linked by a bond to the whole stretch of eternity.' He must have found that a comforting thought as the legions, finally pulling out of Britain, retreated through his diocese and the storm clouds gathered. Even while Britannia was collapsing Victricius crossed the Channel to us, carrying with him relics and so 'enjoying the company of those majestic presences'.

Having such points of contact to heaven available in various localities, no wonder the sick made their way to them seeking tangible contact with eternity. Today, although we have direct access to the Throne, we nevertheless phone our friends and ask them to pray for us in our illnesses. Is it therefore totally illogical that earlier Christians sought the prayers of their own friends who were gone to the divine presence?

There is one thing we forget too easily. In the late twentieth century we turn rightly and first to medical care, to trained doctors with potent drugs, sophisticated tools and skilled surgery. Where could Christians go in the early centuries? They loved their sick children and ailing husbands and dying wives as much as we do ours. This morning I performed a second-stage operation on a young woman who had developed a fast-growing ovarian tumour just after delivery a few months back, and has since had chemotherapy. A thousand years ago, had she been my wife, I would have prayed; but then I would have been on my way hot-foot with her to the tomb of Cuthbert at Chester-le-Street,[23] or of John at Beverley. Well, wouldn't you?

I cannot do better than sum up in the words of Peter Brown:[24]

> The discovery of a relic was far more than an act of pious archeology, and its transfer far more than a strange new form of Christian connoisseurship: both actions made plain at a particular time and place the immensity of God's mercy. They announced moments of amnesty. They brought a sense of deliverance and pardon into the present . . . the relic itself may not have been as important as the invisible gesture of God's forgiveness that it made available in the first place.

There are still places with the sense of the numinous about them: for me the sands of Lindisfarne and the crypt at Hexham. It would be a hard-nosed evangelical protestant who could stand on Friars' Crag at Keswick and remain unconscious of a place heavy with blessing. However to the Christian today, realising he is indwelt by God the Holy Spirit, enjoying the company of the Lord, every place is a site of contact with the one who identified himself as the God who heals you (Exod. 15:26).

The Scots Reformers

Two hundred years ago John Howie[25] wrote: 'The testimony of the Church of Scotland is not only a free, full, and faithful testimony, yea more extensive than the testimony of any one particular church since Christianity commenced in the world, but also a sure and costly testimony, confirmed and sealed with blood.' Even although we may feel that Howie went a little over the top in this estimation, there can be few Christians more admired than those of the kirk in the time it was undergoing persecution. From this period there is more than one account to our purpose: but if these healings, occurring in such a theological climate, can be established, then, even to the most orthodox Protestant, the case for the continuation of miracles must be considered proven. We must therefore look in detail into two of these stories from the first generation of the reformers.

Some Thoughts on Faith Healing[26] refers in passing to an account of John Welch (or Welsh), John Knox's son-in-law, which suggests that he was the means of the resurrection of a young relative. Without further details it quotes a nineteenth-century work, Young's *Life of John Welch*:

> Concerning this youth a tradition was handed down to the effect that, falling sick of a lingering and grievous distemper, he died, but was miraculously brought to life again by the effectual fervent prayer of his affectionate host. This episode, as recorded by Kirkton, is long and minute, but not very edifying. By certain parties it has been made a handle of for casting reproach on the memory of John Welch, on serious religion, and on the cause of Presbytery. . . The amount of the whole, we believe, is simply this – that having a singular care of his young and noble relative, Welch earnestly prayed for his recovery, and it pleased the Sovereign Arbiter of life and death to listen to his supplication for the recovery of the youth when at the point of death.

Because such debunking of miracle accounts is so common it is always worthwhile checking with the primary source. In this case it is to be regretted that the editors of *Some Thoughts on Faith Healing* were misled by a judgment made 250 years after the event. It may be that they did not have access to the extremely elusive Wodrow Society's volume[27] containing the seventeenth-century 'History of Mr John Welsh', which gives a very different picture. This narrative by James Kirkton, who lived a generation later, paints the portrait of a remarkable man of God. Kirkton once asked a former parishioner of Welsh's what sort of man he was, obtaining the answer: 'O sir, he was a type of Christ.' In another contemporary record, Row's *Historie of the Kirk of Scotland*,[28] we read:

> For it is ordinar with God to give his servants whom he

stirres up and employes in extraordinar employments with extraordinar gifts and endewments, such as the gift of prophecie. Such prophets there were many in Scotland, about and shortlie after the tyme of the reformation, viz. Messrs Wishart, Knox, Welsh. . . They foir-prophecied many things, whereof some were fulfilled in their owne dayes, and all of them after their. death.

Of Welsh's prophecies we have room for only one:

While minister in Kirkudbright, he met with a young gallant in scarlet and silver lace come home from his travels, and much surprised the young man by telling him he behoved to change his garb and way of life, and betake himself to the study of Scripture, which at that time was not his business, for he should be his successor in the ministry at Kirkudbright; which accordingly came to pass some time thereafter.[29]

There is more than one demonstration of what we now recognise as the gift of knowledge. At a time of plague the town of Ayr, where Welsh was minister, was free from it, so guards were set at the gates. Two chapmen appeared and produced a pass from the magistrates of the last town, also disease-free. However the Ayr magistrates would not admit them before seeking their minister's advice:

So Mr Welsh was called and his opinion asked. He demurred, and putting off his hat, with his eyes towards heaven for a pretty space, though he uttered no audible words, yet continued in a praying gesture; and after a little space told the magistrates they would do well to discharge those travellers from their town, affirming, with a great asseveration, the plague was in those packs. So the magistrates commanded them to be gone, and they went to Cumnock, a town some twenty miles distant, and there sold their goods which kindled such an infection in that place that the living were hardly able to bury the dead.[30]

Kirkton records[31] of this man, who averaged eight hours a

day in prayer and was exiled for the faith, the incident which we have seen Young refer to as 'not very edifying'. Let the reader judge:

[The patient, the son of Lord Ochiltree, Mrs Welsh's cousin, who had come to stay with them in France] fell sick of a grievous sickness; and after he had long wasted with it, closed his eyes, and expired as dying men do. So to the apprehension and the sense of all spectators he was no more than a carcase, and was therefore taken out of his bed and laid on a pallet on the floor, that his body might be the more conveniently dressed, as dead bodies used to be. This was to Mr Welsh a great grief; and therefore he staid with the young man's body full three hours lamenting over him with great tenderness. After twelve hours friends brought in a coffin, whereinto they desired the corpse to be put, as the custom is. But Mr Welsh desired that, for the satisfaction of his affections, they would forbear the youth for a time, which they granted, and returned not till twenty-four hours after his death were expired.

Then they returned, desiring with great importunity the corpse might be coffined, that it might be speedily buried, the weather being extremely hot; yet he persisted in his request earnestly begging them to excuse him once more: so they left the youth upon his pallet for full thirty-six hours. But even after that, though he was urged, not only with great earnestness, but displeasure, they were constrained to forbear for twelve hours more.

After forty-eight hours were past Mr Welsh was still where he was; and then his friends perceived he believed the young man was not really dead, but under some apopleptic fit, and therefore proponed to him, for his satisfaction, that trial should be made upon his body by doctors and chirurgeons, if possible any spark of life might be found in him; and with this he was content. So the physicians are set to work, who pinched him with pinchers in the fleshy parts of his body, and twisted a bow-string about his head with great force, but no sign of life appeared in him, so the physicians pronounce him stark dead; and then there was no more delay to be desired.

Yet Mr Welsh begged them once more, that they would but step into the next room for an hour or two, and leave him with the dead youth, and this they granted. Then Mr Welsh fell down on the pallet and cried to the Lord with all his might for the last time, till at length the dead youth opened his eyes, and cried out to Mr Welsh, whom he distinctly knew, 'O Sir, I am all whole but my head and my legs' and these were the places they had sore hurt with their pinching. He became an eminent noble in Ireland: Lord Castlesteuart.

It was on account of his tender conscience that John Welsh had been condemned earlier for high treason, and banished; while Kirkton, the recorder of these events, suffered in the later persecutions. No one who reads his book could believe that here are men who would deviate by a hair's breadth from the truth. These are men of whom the world is not worthy.

That this was not a unique case of miraculous healing in those days can be demonstrated from other Lives in the same volume; for instance, from the early 1600s, John Livingstone's account of some of the outstanding ministers he had known personally.[32] One of these was John Scrimger (or Scrimgeour), minister of Kinghorn in Fife, who as royal chaplain went with James VI to Denmark in 1589 to bring back Queen Anne. He was deposed by the same monarch thirty years later, for conscience sake.

'John Scrimger', writes Livingstone, 'was a man rude-like in his clothing and some of his behaviour and expressions, but of a deep reach, and of a natural witt, very learned especially in the Hebrew language . . . one of the most tender loving heart, especially fitted to comfort such as are cast down.' He had lost several children through death, and the only surviving daughter, whom he loved dearly, took

the disease called the King's Evill, or the cruells, and had several running sores, especially one great one in her arm,

85

and was at the point of death, so that one night he was called up to see her die. 'I went out', said he, 'to the fields in the night being in great anxiety, and began to expostulat with God, in a fitt of great displeasure, and said, "Thou knowest, O Lord, I have been serving thee in the uprightness of mine heart, according to my measure, and thou seest I take pleasure in this child, and cannot obtain such a thing as that at thy hand", with other such expressions, as I durst not again utter for all the world, for I was in great bitterness, and at last it was said to me, "I have heard thee at this time, but use not such boldness in time coming, for such particulars"; and I came back, the child was sitting up in bed fully healed, taking some meat, and when I looked at her arm, it was quite healed.'

We turn again to Howie's *Scots Worthies*[33] to read another story of Scrimger which, although not a record of cure of an organic condition, demonstrates his unusual understanding of the Christian's authority:

There was a certain godly woman under his care at Kinghorn who fell sick of a very lingering disease, and was all the while assaulted with strong temptations, leading her to think that she was a castaway, notwithstanding that her whole conversation put the reality of grace in her beyond a doubt. He often visited her while in this deep exercise, but her trouble and terrors still remained. As her dissolution drew on her spiritual trouble increased. He went with two elders to her and began first, in their presence, to comfort and pray with her, but she still grew worse. He ordered his elders to prayer, and afterwards prayed himself, but no relief came.

Then, sitting pensive for a little space, he thus broke silence; 'What is this! Our laying of grounds of comfort before her will not do; prayer will not do; we must try another remedy. Sure I am this is a daughter of Abraham; sure I am she hath sent for me and therefore in the name of God, the Father of our Lord Jesus Christ, who sent Him to redeem sinners; in the name of Jesus Christ who obeyed the Father and came to save us; and in the name of the Holy and blessed Spirit our Quickener and Sanctifier, I, the elder, command thee, a daughter of Abraham, to be loosed from these bonds.' And immediately peace and joy ensued.

Returning to Livingstone,[34] we learn that he visited Scrimger on his death-bed. He was suffering severely from renal colic, crying out bitterly with pain. But there is no word of his seeking for himself the healing he had obtained for others; rather he said to his visitor: 'I have been a rude stunkard (perversley obstinate) man all my dayes, and now by this pain the Lord is dantoning (subduing) me to make me a lamb before he takes me home to himself.'

Raising the dead, healings, prophesyings, words of knowledge: the first generation of the reformed kirk had them all. And more, for we also read in Livingstone of Patrick McLewrath,[35] a godly farmer who often spent whole nights in prayer. Patrick used to meet two friends who had had a similar divine work in their hearts:

> After they had mutually imparted their experience, two of them sitting on a furm, and a third on a chair before the furm, they all took other in their arms, and shook to and again, and uttered their voice in a kind of cruneing singing way, but not uttering any articulate words, and yet the tears running down from them; for at that time they did not understand that there was any such exercise as Christians to pray together.

We have long since learned to pray together, but singing in tongues has only recently been rediscovered.

Some Christians maintain that God manifests himself with miracles only at crucial moments in history. In the biblical record there are clusters of miracles at the Exodus, at the time of the battle by Elijah and Elisha against resurgent heathenism, and at the birth of the Church. Those who hold this theory might be prepared to accept the cases we have been looking at as occurring at similar crucial moments: when the Church was struggling to survive at the collapse of Rome; in the first generation of the evangelisation of the English; and at the Reformation. Those who hold this view maintain that the miraculous gifts of the Spirit are withdrawn between such epochs. Is this borne out by facts?

In Presbyterian Scotland we find continuing evidence of the miraculous gifts of the Spirit. For the eighteenth century we can turn to the Synod of Ross volume in the authoritative series, *Fasti Ecclesiae Scoticanae*.[36] Under the parish of Resolis, in place of the normal mere list of names of ministers, we read:

> Hector McPhail, who held the charge from 1746 to 1774, 'was one of the most deeply exercised Christians of his time'. His help was sought for a woman violently insane. Going to her he prayed, 'O Thou who are three times holy, I implore Thee not to allow me to rise from my knees should they rot to earth, until Thou makest it visibly known here that there is a God in Israel.' The prayer was speedily heard and answered, as before the pious and godly man rose from his prostrations the patient was loosed from her bonds, and so calmed and restored that she sat up and conversed with him and the others in a sound mind, giving glory to God.

Bede[37] has an almost identical story of the healing, through Cuthbert, of a similarly afflicted wife of a similar godly man, eleven centuries earlier. God does not lapse into inactivity.

McPhail also had the gift of knowledge. Seated one day at dinner in the house of a parishioner he suddenly rose from table, left the house and hurried into a nearby wood. Hidden within it was a small lake, on the edge of which he found a woman just about to drown herself. He was able to dissuade her and reconcile her to God. Turning to the nineteenth century we note this same gift recorded, in *The Days of the Fathers in Ross-shire*,[38] by a Free Kirk minister, John Kennedy. He tells of his own father who, in full health, planned and delivered a series of farewell addresses in the knowledge that he would be dead in a few days. What is this, mere premonition? No, for I have stood by his gravestone and read with awe: 'He was a man through whom shone the excellency of the power. . . The ministerial gifts and graces of primitive times . . . in his person were seen realised.'

We have covered the planned ground, but let us look at a case of healing in the life of one of the great English Christians of the seventeenth century, the puritan divine Richard Baxter. He had a throat tumour which disappeared at the moment when, overcoming his inhibitions and modesty, he proclaimed God's healing powers. He records the incident in *The Saint's Everlasting Rest*:[39]

> I had a tumour, round like a pease, and at first no bigger; and at last no bigger than a small button, and hard like a bone. The fear lest it should prove to be a cancer troubled me more than the thing itself. I used first dissolving medicines, and then lenient for palliation, and all in vain, for about a quarter of a year. At last my conscience smote me for silencing so many former deliverances, that I had had in answer to prayers; merely in pride lest I should be derided as making ostentation of God's special mercies to myself, as if I were a special favourite of heaven, I made no public mention of them.
>
> I was that morning to preach on 'eminent providences'. In obedience to my conscience I said: 'How many times have I known the prayer of faith to save the sick when all physicians have given them up for dead. It has been my own case more than once or twice or ten times, when means have all failed, and the highest art of reason has sentenced me hopeless, yet have I been relieved by the prevalence of prevailing prayer.'
>
> When I went to church that morning I had my tumour as before (for I frequently saw it in the glasse, and felt it constantly). As soon as I had done preaching, I felt it was gone, and hastening to the glasse, I saw that there was not the least vestigium or cicatrix, or mark wherever it had

89

been: nor did I at all discover what had become of it. I am sure I neither swallowed it nor spit it out, and it was unlikely to dissolve by any natural cause, that had been hard like bone a quarter of a year, notwithstanding dissolving gargarismes. I thought it fit to mention this, because it was done just as I spoke the words here written.

It is obvious that Baxter believed God had healed his tumour as a reward for his testimony; although an alternative explanation might be that his previous failure to testify had held up his healing. It is worth observing that his testimony was not only to his own previous healings, but to the many other cases he had known.

These records reproduced from the literature, and those I report for the first time, are merely the tip of the iceberg. In vew of this (always provided that we are prepared to adopt the ordinary criteria of evidence which we employ and accept in everyday life) it is surely impossible to maintain any longer that healing miracles have ever ceased in the experience of the Church.

1. Sulpicius Severus, 'Life of St Martin', in A. Roberts, *Nicene and Post-Nicene Fathers*, 2nd ser., vol. XI (1898), pp. 3–17. A more recent translation is by F. H. Hoare, *The Western Fathers*. London, Sheed & Ward 1954.
2. C. Stancliffe, *St Martin and his Hagiographer: history and miracle in Sulpicius Severus*. Oxford, Clarendon Press 1983.
3. J. A. Duke, *The Columban Church*. OUP 1932; repr. Edinburgh, Oliver & Boyd 1957.
4. Sulpicius Severus, 'Three Letters of St Martin and Two Dialogues', tr. F. H. Hoare, *The Western Fathers*.
5. C. ten Boom and J. and E. Sherrill, *The Hiding Place*. London, Hodder & Stoughton 1972.
6. M. Maddocks, *The Christian Healing Ministry*. London, SPCK 1981.
7. D. Bridge, *Signs and Wonders Today* (London, IVP 1985), pp. 160–3.
8. A. C. Fryer, *Aidan the Apostle of England*. London, Partridge 1902.
9. *Bede's Ecclesiastical History of the English People*, ed. B. Colgrave and R. A. B. Mynors. Oxford, Clarendon Press 1969.
10. *Two Lives of St Cuthbert*, ed. B. Colgrave. Cambridge University Press

1940. Includes 'Bede's Prose Life', and 'A Life by an Anonymous Monk of Lindisfarne'.

11. 'Bede's Prose Life of St Cuthbert', ch. 30, in ibid. See also n. 13.

12. The most sympathetic treatment of Wilfrid is H. Mayr-Harting, *The Coming of Christianity to Anglo-Saxon England*. London, Batsford 1972; and D. P. Kirby, *St Wilfrid at Hexham*. Newcastle upon Tyne, Oriel Press 1974.

13. *The Life of Bp Wilfrid by Eddius Stephanus*, ed. B. Colgrave. Cambridge University Press 1927. Eddius, and 'Bede's Prose Life of St Cuthbert', are also tr. J. G. Webb, in D. H. Farmer (ed.) *The Age of Bede*. London, Penguin 1983.

14. B. Schlink, *Realities: the miracles of God experienced today*. London, Marshall 1967.

15. *Bede's Ecclesiastical History*, III.1–6.

16. F. Arnold-Forster, *Studies in Church Dedications or England's patron saints*. London, Skeffington 1899.

17. R. Foster, *Meditative Prayer*. London, Marc 1983.

18. P. Clemoes, *The Cult of St Oswald on the Continent*, 1983 Jarrow Lecture. St Paul's Church, Jarrow.

19. E. P. Baker, 'St Oswald and his church at Zug', *Archaeologia*, 93 (1949), pp. 102–23; and 'The cult of St Oswald in N. Italy', ibid. 94 (1951), pp. 167–94.

20. R. Finucane, *Miracles and Pilgrims: popular belief in mediaeval England*. London, Dent 1977.

21. *Letters and Papers . . . of the Reign of Henry VIII*, XIV, p. 155, qu. in T. M. Lindsay, *A History of the Reformation*, vol. II (Edinburgh, Clark 1906), p. 344.

22. P. Brown, *The Cult of the Saints*. London, SCM 1981.

23. The calumny that St Cuthbert was a misogynist, and women could not go to his shrine, was not foisted on the public until the eleventh century. See V. Tudor, in *Archeologia Aeliana*, 12 (1984), pp. 157–68.

24. P. Brown, p. 92.

25. J. Howie, *The Scots Worthies*. 1781; reissued Edinburgh, Johnstone, Hunter 1870.

26. V. Edmunds and C. G. Scorer (eds), *Some Thoughts on Faith Healing*, 3rd rev. edn. London, CMF 1979.

27. J. Kirkton, 'The history of Mr John Welsh', in *Select Biographies* (Edinburgh, Wodrow Soc. 1845), vol. I, pp. 1–62.

28. J. Row, *Historie of the Kirk of Scotland*. Edinburgh, Wodrow Soc. 1842.

29. Kirkton, p. 4.

30. ibid. pp. 12–13.

31. ibid. pp. 35–7.

32. J. Livingstone, in *Select Biographies* (Wodrow Soc.), vol. I, p. 308.

33. Howie, pp. 115–18.

34. Livingstone, p. 309.

35. ibid. pp. 337–8.
36. H. Scott (ed.), *Fasti Ecclesiae Scoticanae*. Edinburgh 1915.
37. *Bede's Ecclesiastical History*.
38. J. Kennedy, *The Days of the Fathers in Ross-shire*. n.d.; reissued Inverness, Christian Focus Publications 1979.
39. R. Baxter, *The Saint's Everlasting Rest*, II.vi.5 (many edns).

5

A New Pentecost?

In Chapter 4 we noted that since the close of the apostolic age healings have occurred in three forms: there are men like Martin and Cuthbert possessing recognised God-given healing powers; there are the repeated healings at places associated with godly men or women, such as King Oswald; and scattered through the centuries many 'one-off' healings in answer to prayer.

But despite all this the experience of the Church is far inferior to that recorded as the norm in the Acts of the Apostles. The tide of power had gone a long way out. One morning I walked on our superb sands watching the tide returning in a series of waves, each coming farther up the beach. Just so can we identify a series of waves of the Holy Spirit in the last 150 years or so. I will spotlight three of the many.

1830: Firth of Clyde[1]

One of those dissatisfied with the poverty of the Church's experience was the Revd Edward Irving,[2] since 1822 minister of the National Scotch Church in London. He wrote:

Today the gifts of the Spirit are not looked for . . . I am one (of those) who feel the bondage of this system; and wait on Divine Providence for a call and the work of the Spirit for a warrant to restore to the Church its ancient liberty. And I believe I shall not wait long, when it shall please the Holy Ghost to furnish men with gifts to fit them for apostles, prophets, evangelists, discerners of spirits, speakers with tongues and interpreters of tongues.

When he visited the Firth of Clyde in 1828, among those influenced by his teaching, and by the evangelical preaching of his friend the Revd Macleod Campbell of Rhu, were two sisters, Isabella and Mary Campbell of Ferincarry. Isabella, whose saintly life gathered a circle round her, was soon dead, and her sister bedridden. The latter was suffering 'from a disease which the medical men pronounced to be a decline and would soon bring her to her grave whither her sister Isabella had been hurried by the same malady some months earlier'.

One Sunday evening in March 1830 some friends had gone to Mary Campbell's bedroom to pray with her, having spent the day 'in humiliation, and fasting, and prayer before God, with a special respect to the restoration of the gifts'. In the midst of their devotions by her sofa the Holy Spirit came with such power on Mary that she spoke at great length and with superhuman strength in an unknown tongue, to the astonishment of all who heard. A few days later she was constrained by the Spirit 'to go and ask the Father, in the name of Jesus, to stretch forth His hand to heal . . . to ask in faith, nothing doubting'.

We will leave Mary Campbell there for the moment, and cross the Firth to Port Glasgow where the Macdonald family lived: James and George who worked in a shipyard, and their two unmarried sisters, one of whom, Margaret, was very ill. It seems that Margaret Macdonald, like the Campbell sisters, was suffering from 'galloping consumption', pulmonary tuberculosis, which we have already seen killing Thérèse of Lisieux, and which would cut down many more young women, among them some of my own teenage acquaintances. The Macdonald family, whose only reading was the Bible, attended the parish church and had not been subject to the fervent preaching which elsewhere was causing such a stir, and was to stimulate a heresy hunt. One day the same March two friends were sitting by Margaret's bedside. She had been so weak that it had hardly been possible to make the bed for several days.

Suddenly she said, 'There will be a mighty baptism of the Spirit this day!' and broke forth in a most marvellous setting forth of the wonderful work of God; and as if her own weakness had been altogether lost in the strength of the Holy Ghost, continued with little or no intermission for two or three hours in mingled praise, prayer, and exhortation. It was assumed that she was dying and this accounted for the singular exhibition. However when her brothers came in for dinner she addressed them at great length, concluding with a solemn prayer for James that he might at that time be endowed with the Holy Ghost.

Almost instantly James said calmly, 'I have got it.' He walked to the window and stood silent for a moment or two. I looked at him and almost trembled, there was such a change in his whole countenance. He then with a step and manner of the most indescribable majesty, walked to Margaret's bedside.

James addressed her in words from the metrical Psalm 20, 'Rise and upright stand'. He repeated the words, took her by the hand, and she arose. The family record closes with the matter-of-fact phrase: 'We all sat quietly down and took our dinner.' That afternoon James wrote to Mary Campbell commanding her in the name of the Lord to arise.

We can now return to Ferincarry where Mary Campbell had been constrained to pray for healing.

It was not long after that I received James Macdonald's letter. . . As I read every word came with power, but when I came to the command to rise, it came home with a power no words can describe; it was felt to be indeed the word of Christ . . . such a voice of power as could not be resisted. . .

The next day James Macdonald demonstrated the reality of his faith by going down to the quay to meet Miss Campbell if she came over the water. 'The result showed how much he knew of what God had done, and would do for her, for she came as he expected, declaring herself perfectly whole.'

These events, unique in the contemporary experience of the churches of the day, caused a furore, which a few months later was exacerbated by the affair of Miss Fancourt, the daughter of a clergyman in London. She had suffered from increasing hip disease from 1822 to 1828, thereafter becoming a helpless cripple. One evening in 1830, in response to prayer, she was healed. By the end of a week she could walk more than a mile. She wrote, 'I am perfectly well. To Jesus be all the glory.'

We may say that if the Holy Spirit fathered these manifestations in 1830 the ecclesiastical midwives did their best to stifle them at birth. For all practical purposes they succeeded. Infanticide was preferable to allowing such an abnormal infant into the family. But let us not be too critical, it is how most of use would react when our personal security is threatened. We are managing to ride the seas of life on an even keel, and if anyone rocks the boat our immediate response is to shout at them to sit down and be quiet. This is especially true in the deepest spiritual areas of our life. We have all done it.

If we dissect it the response to the 'Irvingites', both then and now, as well as our negative response to the case histories in this book, is dictated by fear. Fear for our professional credibility, for our standing in Christian circles, and more important, fear of the unknown. We have got things buttoned up, we know where we are, our intellects are in firm control – what on earth might happen if we let this thing in? Might not our brains be overridden while we gabble incoherently or find ourselves swinging from the chandeliers and dancing in the aisles? Heaven forfend.

So our reaction is to pick holes in the experience and behaviour of the witnesses. And of course it is child's play to do so. In medicine or in any new enterprise, on the initiation of a new technique or the discovery of some new advance, do we ever get it exactly right the first time? Of course not. It takes years of experimentation and discussion to enter into its full value. But we do not knock the pioneers. I am not suggesting that the Holy Spirit did not give his gifts perfectly from the beginning, but that our use and understanding of them requires time and discussion. Even this book is a part of the ongoing discussion of his gifts of healing.

So the Campbell sisters were mercilessly dissected. Mary is the frontrunner, perhaps the first believer in modern times to be recognised as speaking in tongues. Apart from the New Testament record she had nothing to go on, she got some of it wrong, believing eventually that she had been given a language for missionary service. James Macdonald gives a prophecy, which is shown to bear resemblance to something in the press, and is brow-beaten into thinking he had imagined it all. The undoubted difficulties in Edward Irving's church in London are raked over, and he is made to appear a rather pathetic failure; a judgment denied by David Ker, one of his church officers, in a fascinating pamphlet.[3] The word Ker uses is not 'failure' but – significantly in our present situation – 'restoration'. A more recent historian[4] likewise has a positive estimation of Irving's ministry.

> Sixty years (after his deposition) in partial reparation, the Moderator of the General Assembly, Professor A. M. Carteris, unveiled a statue of him in Annan. There, beside the parish kirk in which he was ordained in 1822 and deposed in 1833, stands the representation of that courageous, single-minded man who in so brief a ministry served with such tireless devotion the Kirk he loved and the Master he owned.

Of Miss Fancourt's healing the *Christian Observer*[5] wrote: 'We must admit any solution rather than miracle.' Everyone closed ranks. By 1834 the Scots church historian Thomas McCrie, whose *Life of John Knox* was a best-seller, could write: 'If I were to treat the subject afresh, I would perhaps be disposed to interpose more cautions against the danger of mistaking the impressions of a heated imagination for supernatural communications. The extravagant pretensions . . . in our own day show the dangers of this extreme. . .'[6]

97

So by one means or another we manage to prove to our own satisfaction that this talk of miraculous gifts of the Spirit is all a ghastly mistake. Bingo! we are relieved from the terror of actually having to deal with an active God the Holy Spirit. We are quite happy to forgive David his affair with Bathsheba, and continue to revel in the Psalms; Peter's betrayal, and later cowardly backsliding in front of the Judaists, can be overlooked leaving his status unimpaired – because they do not threaten us. But these folk do, so let us undermine their reputations at all costs.

With hindsight, the events on Clydeside, despite the mistakes, were the first streaks heralding the dawn of God's new Pentecost. We are going to have to do a lot of apologising in heaven.

1907: Yorkshire

As the tide comes in the next wave to watch is Smith Wigglesworth.[7] When you have smiled at the name, you will probable fail to find it in the index of most mainstream texts. His biography however, by Stanley Frodsham, is so amazing that I was relieved to have Edward Bairstow, a family doctor in practice near Bradford, to assure me that his parents knew Smith Wigglesworth well, and that the stories are not exaggerated.

Wigglesworth was born of humble parents in West Yorkshire in 1859, and started work at the age of six. Although he could never recollect a time when he did not long for God, he was converted two years later at a revival meeting in a Wesleyan Methodist church. Eager to give his testimony he would always break down and weep, until one evening three old men who knew him intimately came over to where he was weeping unable to speak, and laid their hands on him. 'Immediately the Spirit of the Lord came upon me and I was instantly set free from my bondage. I not only believed, but I could also speak.' At nine he was confirmed:

I can still remember when the Bishop laid his hands on

me I had a similar experience to the one I had forty years later when I was baptised in the Holy Spirit. My whole body was filled with the consciousness of God's presence, a consciousness that remained with me for days.

When the Salvation Army came to Bradford Wigglesworth, now sixteen, met them for it seemed to him that they had more power in their ministry than anyone else at that time. 'We used to have all-nights of prayer. Many would be laid out under the power of the Spirit, sometimes for as long as twenty-four hours. We called that the Baptism in the Spirit in those days.' At twenty he moved to Liverpool 'and the power of God was mightily upon me . . . I fasted all day every Sunday and prayed, and I never remember seeing less than fifty souls saved by the Power of God in the meetings with the children, in hospitals, on ships, and in the Salvation Army.'

Back in Bradford he discovered a divine healing meeting-place in nearby Leeds. There was such reality in these meetings, where the Lord was healing people, that he began to hunt out sick people in Bradford and pay their fare to Leeds. In his own mission-hall they painted a scroll behind the platform: 'I am the Lord that healeth thee' (Exod. 15:26 av). However he was challenged by his wife for his own lack of faith, in that having haemorrhoids he used laxatives daily. So he went to the loo, anointed himself with oil (Jas. 5:14) and had no further trouble.

Hearing of a Christian woman who was dying he took two godly friends with him to pray for her. These friends prayed for the husband so soon to be bereaved and for the children who would be motherless. But Wigglesworth had hidden a half-pint bottle of oil in his pocket:

I pulled the cork out of the bottle, and went over to the dying woman. I was a novice at this time and did not know any better, so I poured all the contents over Mrs Clark's body in the name of Jesus! I was standing at the top of the bed and looking towards the foot, and suddenly the Lord Jesus appeared. I had my eyes open gazing at Him. There

He was at the foot of the bed. He gave me one of those gentle smiles. . . After a few minutes He vanished but something happened that day that changed my whole life. Mrs Clark was raised up and filled with life for many years.

Having heard preaching on 'entire sanctification' he prayed for ten days. 'God surely did something for me . . . we counted that as the Baptism of the Spirit.'

He and his wife agreed never to use medicines, and two of their children when ill were instantly healed. He himself was moribund with appendicitis so they called the doctor (not for treatment against their principles but to avoid a coroner's inquest becoming necessary). The doctor stated that he was too weak for operation which would have been his only hope, and said he would call back later. When he did so shortly afterwards, Wigglesworth was out at work. Two friends had laid hands on him and prayed, upon which he felt as well as he had ever been in his life, so got up and resumed his employment as a plumber.

In 1907 the modern pentecostal movement reached Britain, beginning in Sunderland at All Saints Church, Monkwearmouth. (On the outside wall of the church hall are still engraved the words: 'The Fire Fell and Burned up the Debt'.) When news of this reached Bradford Wigglesworth decided to go to Monkwearmouth as he was anxious to see this thing – it was the 'speaking in tongues' which drew him. He was disappointed not to receive that gift, and admitted as much when he went to the vicarage to say goodbye. Mrs Boddy, the vicar's wife, said, 'It's not tongues you need, but the Baptism.' Wigglesworth replied, 'I have received the baptism, sister, but I would like you to lay hands on me before I leave. He reported later:

> The fire fell . . . I was there with God alone. He bathed me in power. . . I was given a vision in which I saw the Lord Jesus Christ. I beheld the empty cross, and I saw Him exalted . . . I could speak no longer in English but I began to praise Him in other tongues as the Spirit of God gave me utterance. I knew then, although I might have

received anointings previously, that now I had received the real Baptism in the Holy Spirit as they received on the day of Pentecost.

Following this he had a world-wide ministry with a vast number of healings. Typically he would say at a meeting: 'The first person in this large audience who stands up, whatever his or her sickness, I'll pray for that one and God will deliver him or her.' His certainty is breathtaking.

I have recorded the earliest part of Smith Wigglesworth's story in some detail because it demonstrates, better than any other, the crucial step in the argument. Here was a Christian, godly, zealous, blessed in his ministry, sanctified, with experience of God healing bodily diseases, in whom we see all the strands of the spiritual life and the healing ministry brought together. Then he entered into the experience of the disciples as recorded in Acts 2, and of the New Testament Church, and all the pieces fell into place. It was all suddenly integrated. This is the situation many churches are reaching in the last quarter of the twentieth century, which was then only beginning.

It will be noted that in Britain the first experiences were in an Anglican parish, but soon the establishments rallied round and the pentecostals were quarantined – very effectively. It was to be half a century before, partly through their witness, the Holy Spirit was allowed to pour out his gifts on the mainstream denominations.

1959: California

The story of the next decades can be conveniently read in *As at the Beginning* by Michael Harper,[8] a frontrunner in England. There were many waves creeping up the shores, but I have chosen 1959 for in that year Dennis Bennett,[9] vicar of an Episcopal church in California, entered into a totally new experience of the Holy Spirit, as did a number of his congregation within a short time. One day his son was going to miss a party because he had scratched his eye and it was too sore. 'Without thinking too much about it,' records Bennett, 'I put my hand on his head and prayed under my breath.' Shortly afterwards he was astonished when his wife said, 'Funny thing, he's perfectly OK. His eye suddenly stopped hurting him, and he's going to the party after all.' Bennett asked himself a question which is central to our study: healing, was this 'part of the package' too?

Previously like many other churches they had had weekly 'healing services', and Bennett reckoned that they prayed for at least a thousand people a year to be healed of one ailment or another. They had had healing missions, even getting a well-known leader over from England. Hundreds had come to hear, and to the altar rail for prayer. On the last night his wife had said, 'It's been wonderful, and I know a lot of people have been helped and encouraged, but – where are the healings?' Now however things were different. One of the church members came for prayer for the ugly eczema or psoriasis which covered her hands. 'I wish', wrote Bennett, 'I had not looked away for a moment, for when I looked back the unsightly lesions were all gone. The skin was as clear as a baby's.'

Healing as an integral part, almost a by-product, of spiritual renewal is the discovery of many Christians today, as demonstrated by the following case, which was brought to my attention by a friend who has known the patient for a number of years.

CASE RECORD 5.1

Miss M., a teacher, underwent a hysterectomy in 1982. Thereafter for three months she had severe hip pain, which then became somewhat less, but following that there was no further improvement. She had been a great walker but now she found that after walking some distance she would limp. She could not cross her right leg over her left without pain. She had to buy a new mattress to obtain comfort in bed.

In June 1985 she went with a church party to a meeting for spiritual renewal in a neighbouring church, not with any thought of healing but because she was anxious to hear one of the speakers. During the course of the service another of the speakers made a series of specific comments including: 'There is someone here with trouble in their right hip.' At first Miss M. merely wondered vaguely to whom this might be addressed. She suddenly realised it referred to herself. She raised her hand, whereupon prayer was offered.

When I met her for the first time in 1985 she informed me that since that moment she has had no further trouble at all, can walk, cross her legs without discomfort, and has discarded the special mattress.

A trivial case we may think, but not to the patient.

I have quoted Dennis Bennett's experiences not because they were different from many others which can now be found in scores of books, but because this was the beginning in the mainstream denominations. They did not know; it was all discovery. Now this renewal in the Holy Spirit is the experience of tens of millions of Christians (and I mention the figure with due care) and many thousands of churches of every denomination. Therein, of course, is the rub. That God the Holy Spirit is choosing to manifest himself in churches which are not true-blue by our own particular definition is upsetting. God's carelessness of our criteria of orthodoxy is a distress to many who sit checking over the defences of the theological bunkers in which we have all been accustomed to shelter. In our dilemma we ask, can this really be the work of God?

The dilemma occasioned by miraculous healing can be illustrated from the work of the brilliant expositor and scholar B. B. Warfield (1851–1921), whose arguments against the genuineness of any renewal of the charismata we will consider in Chapter 7. In a discussion on Lourdes[10] he recorded some of the more amazing cures in detail, and was prepared to admit them inexplicable. For instance, of Pierre de Rudder's suppurating wound which healed instantly, Warfield wrote:

We are willing to believe it happened just as it is said to have happened. We are content to know that, in no case, was it a miracle. . . Even although we should stand dumb before the wonders of Lourdes, and should be utterly incapable of suggesting a natural causation for them, we know right well that they are not of God. The whole complex of circumstances of which they are part; their origin in occurrences the best that can be said of which is that they are silly; their intimate connection with a cult derogatory to the rights of God who alone is to be called upon in our distresses, stamp them, prior to all examination of the mode of their occurrences as not from God. . . That God is one, and that He alone is to be served with religious veneration, is no doubt an old revelation. It is nevertheless a true revelation. And he who takes it as such can never believe that miracles are wrought at Lourdes. . . 'The whole place', says Benson, 'is alive with Mary'. That is the reason why we are sure that the marvels are not the direct acts of God.

Presumably Warfield would have rejected the following case out of hand, a course I cannot follow, knowing something of the spiritual status of the persons involved. It was brought to my notice by a relative of the patient and I have been able to discuss both the medical and spiritual aspects with the family doctor. In view of the nature of the case it is perhaps worth mentioning that these two witnesses are both conservative evangelicals very active in the Lord's work.

CASE RECORD 5.2

The patient is an insulin-dependent diabetic whose teaching-hospital records go back to 1971. Around 1975 he and his wife, both devout Roman Catholics, became involved in the Renewal and started to attend house groups, both interdenominational (where I met them) and within their own communion.

In 1976 he suffered a small stroke. On 15 April that year he had his first myocardial infarction, a second in

December, and a third in April 1977, with confirmatory (transaminase) tests. A consultant physician wrote: 'In view of his past history of heart failure and diabetes the prospect for therapy to improve this man is depressing.' By this stage he could not even reach the garden, and then further deteriorated so as to be completely bedridden for seven months. He was diagnosed as having a massive ventricular aneurysm. At this time a research project within the Royal College of General Practitioners was under consideration aimed at investigating the possibility of cardiac surgery in patients with crippling chest pain. In this connection this patient's records and ECGs were reviewed by two professorial assessors, who concurred with the diagnosis.

One night in 1979 the family doctor had to tell him that he was probably dying, and told his wife that he would probably do so that night. However he survived and in the morning a priest came and conducted a service in the bedroom. During the Eucharist the sense of God's presence was so real that they could not move. The patient said: 'I'm not lying on the bed, He's got His arms round me.' Eventually his wife went downstairs to prepare some food and returned to find her husband standing looking out of the window. The GP said: 'Stop the tablets, they are not doing any good. God is looking after him.' From then on the patient could walk as far as the bottom of the garden, but for anything further required a wheeled chair.

Shortly after this they attended the ordination to the priesthood of a friend. When at the end of the service the new priest laid his hands in blessing on the patient's head, the latter was aware of new power. On reaching home he was able to walk upstairs without difficulty. This advance was maintained.

One night at her devotions, as his wife shut her eyes they appeared to be looking into a lighted room which she recognised as Lourdes. On opening her eyes she was back in her own bedroom, but when she closed them the same picture reappeared. However the idea that they should go to Lourdes held no appeal whatever. (In conversation with the author she expressed herself very forcefully on this point.) Lourdes was no doubt all right for some pious folk, and she had a devotion to Mary, but now they 'believed in going to the Top'. God could heal them just as well in north-east England as in Lourdes. 'It was the last place we wanted to go.' She did not even mention this to her husband for some weeks, and when she did, he too was not very keen. In any case they had no money available for the trip. Shortly after, unexpectedly, she was told that the local branch of the Society of St Vincent de Paul would like to send them to Lourdes. She demurred. 'We really feel we should send you. We know your husband won't go without you.' She replied reluctantly, 'Well, we won't take money for both of us. If God really wants us to go He'll have to send money for one of us from somewhere else.'

Some days later a visitor to their home, who knew nothing of the suggested trip, thrust a cheque of the right size into their hands.

On arrival at Lourdes men and women go to separate ice-cold baths. When they met afterwards it proved that they had each had very similar experiences, stepping out bone dry (so that no towel was needed) and full of praise. The patient has not used a wheelchair since, he is holding down a full-time active job. He had in fact been involved in the building of the Health Centre where, later, I went over his clinical details with the family doctor. He is still a diabetic but on visiting hospital in 1982 he saw a different consultant physician who commented: 'This man has no real evidence at all of cardiac problems.'

There are a number of points worthy of note. Any quibbling about the exact cardiological diagnosis is of no importance, as without any doubt he was a cardiac invalid *in extremis*. First we notice that while the major problem – his heart condition – was completely cured, his diabetes remained. Secondly we see that the healing was not instantaneous but occurred in a series of stages. Thirdly we find that the final step occurred in circumstances uncongenial both to the patient and his wife. We are irresistibly reminded again of the incident where the general Naaman, suffering from leprosy, is told to go and dip in the Jordan, a dirty foreign stream. We can understand his annoyance: 'Are not Abana and Pharpar, rivers of Damascus, better than all the waters of Israel? May I not wash in them and be clean?' (2 Kings 5:10–12 AV). And we stand alongside the ex-patient and his wife in believing that God is as real and active in our home towns as he is at the end of a pilgrimage. Yet, in their case, *pace* Warfield, that was the way God wanted it.

God does not work according to a template. We note this in conversion. Although classically in some traditions it is seen in terms of an understanding of the '3 Rs': Ruin (our state, through sin), Righteousness (required by God) and Redemption (achieved for us, by Christ); it has been experienced by Christians in many different ways. Take C. S. Lewis:[11]

> You must picture me alone in that room in Magdalen, night after night, feeling, whenever my mind lifted even for a second from my work, the steady, unrelenting approach of Him whom I so earnestly desired not to meet. That which I greatly feared had at last come upon me. In the Trinity Term of 1929 I gave in and admitted that God was God, and knelt and prayed: perhaps that night the most dejected and reluctant convert in all England. I did not see then what is the most shining and obvious thing; the Divine humility which will accept a convert even on such terms. But who can duly adore that Love which will open the high gates to a prodigal who is brought in kicking, struggling, resentful, and darting his eyes in every direction for a chance to escape?

Similarly initiation into the rediscovered life of the Holy Spirit is in some cases dramatic, and in others of us gentle, without any overt manifestations. Which is what we might expect comparing Acts 2 with 1 Corinthians 12–14.

In Jesus' own healing ministry we see the same absence of

any protocol. Agreed that some differences between his cases were due to his spiritual diagnostic skill – this one first forgiven of sin, that one requiring the casting out of demons, the others straightforward cases of organic disease. But other differences in Jesus' therapeutic technique we cannot explain. Why make clay and anoint the diseased organ for one, just touch another, merely say the word for a third, and heal the fourth *in absentia*? Surely, as in the Co. Durham case just described (p. 104), he individualises the management according to his own wisdom. We must not try to stereotype God's work, least of all make acceptance of it conditional on its falling within the bounds of *our* presuppositions and *our* historic bulwarks.

A very large number of cases of healing are now being recorded in the literature of the renewal – which Cardinal Suenens has called the 'Second Pentecost'. Some of these are no doubt exaggerated, a few may even be fraudulent. The vast majority – although no less appreciated by the sufferers on this account – are of conditions which can be classified as psychosomatic.

When all these have been set aside, we find that the kind of healings seen in Palestine during the ministry of our Lord Jesus are being seen again in the last decades of this century. And these healings are not in isolation but an integral aspect of spiritual renewal. Such statements are easy to make, but will they stand up to examination? We must turn to that next.

---

1. When I wrote this part I did not have available Dr Gordon Strachan's *The Pentecostal Theology of Edward Irving* (London, Darton, Longman and Todd 1973), which splendid work is mandatory reading for the subject of this chapter.
2. For Edward Irving, see *Letters of Thomas Erskine of Linlathern*, ed. W. Hanna. Edinburgh, Douglas 1878; and A. L. Drummond, *Edward Irving and his Circle*. London, James Clarke n.d. The standard biography is by Mrs Oliphant, 2 vols. London 1862.
3. D. Ker, *Observations on Mrs Oliphant's 'Life of Edward Irving' and correction*

of certain mis-statements therein. Edinburgh, Thos Laurie 1863. A copy, bound with Mrs Oliphant's Life, 1 vol. edn, is in the Evangelical Library.

4. G. G. Cameron, *The Scots Kirk in London*. Oxford, Becket 1969.
5. *Christian Observer*, qu. in A. J. Gordon, *The Ministry of Healing*. London, Hodder & Stoughton 1886.
6. Thomas McCrie, letter dated 1834 to W. H. Carslaw's father, who quotes from it in his preface to his edition of Howie's *Scots Worthies* (see p. 91 n. 25).
7. S. H. Frodsham, *Smith Wigglesworth: apostle of faith*. Nottingham, Assemblies of God 1949.
8. M. Harper, *As at the Beginning*. London, Hodder & Stoughton 1965.
9. D. J. Bennett, *Nine o'Clock in the Morning*. Eastbourne, Kingsway 1971.
10. B. B. Warfield, *Counterfeit Miracles* (1918; reissued Edinburgh, Banner of Truth 1972), pp. 118–21.
11. C. S. Lewis, *Surprised by Joy* (London, Bles 1955), p. 215.

6

The Biblical Basis for Miracles

The Approach to Scripture

Let me start by laying my cards on the table. I assume that the Bible records are meant to be taken in their straightforward meaning. 'Other Christians', wrote Bishop Hensley Henson half a century ago (obviously including himself):

> will take another course. To them this naively uncritical handling of Scripture will be impossible... They will find the key to the evangelists' records in the facts of psychotherapy and the teachings of psychology ... the miracles of Jesus Christ are seen to form no exception to the normal experience of mankind, but only to be supreme illustrations of phenomena which are co-terminous with human life.[1]

The many different viewpoints can be seen in *Miracles and the Critical Mind*,[2] where Colin Brown examines the attitude to miracles of some 800 authorities. Those interested should start by using Brown's magnificent volume as an index to the literature. However here we must press on to the New Testament itself, for although there are Old Testament examples we have no time to examine them.

But note my earlier word 'straightforward'. The idea frequently surfaces that the Bible can really only be understood by use of some special and often esoteric tool, some special approach.

On one side we are told of a school of thought which holds that only those of Paul's epistles written after 'the mystery' (the Church) had been revealed to him are really appropriate to the Church age; hence his earlier letters to the Thessalonians, Corinthians, Galatians and Romans must be of only limited applicability to us today.

Again, a much respected Bible teacher[3] has denied that Pentecost is the birthday of the Church, holding that the earlier events recorded in the Acts were a second (but unaccepted) offer of the Messiah to Israel, and therefore irrelevant to the Church age.

At the other end of the spectrum are those who suggest that the latest tools of biblical criticism are mandatory for an adequate interpretation of the biblical documents, and teach that proper understanding demands linguistic skills in New Testament Greek and, more important, theological German.

If these views are correct then our hearts must bleed for the seventy or more generations who have got it wrong. We must pity Aidan – to whom more than any other single person we in England owe the evangelisation of our land – and those who accompanied him who 'whether tonsured or laymen, had to engage in some form of study, that is to say to occupy themselves with reading the scriptures or learning the psalms'.[4] We must sympathise with his successor John Wesley, ceaselessly travelling round Britain, reading the Scriptures as he rode, and – on this view – inevitably misunderstanding them. Must we believe that they, and the countless other godly people who for almost 2000 years have relied on the Bible, have in fact been stumbling about in the dark, misunderstanding God's message to them because of their ignorance of 'dispensational truth' or of 'the assured findings of contemporary scholarship'?

It is true that each generation sees some truth with particular clarity – our own reads Peter's prophetic words 'the elements shall melt with fervent heat' (2 Peter 3:10 AV) with a horrified insight mercifully denied to our pre-Hiroshima ancestors. The light shed by exegetes and scholars is, of course, invaluable. Nevertheless every generation, and every community – primitive as well as sophisticated, eastern as well as western – must find the Bible to mean what it plainly says as they read it with their contemporary understanding guided by the Holy Spirit. That final clause is the vital one. So they are correct who claim that a special tool is necessary rightly to understand Scripture. That tool proves to be a person – God the Holy Spirit himself who has been promised to guide us into all truth (John 16:13).

All miracles the work of the Spirit. It might also be well, at the outset, to state the thesis I maintain in this chapter. It is that all healing miracles are the work of God the Holy Spirit, whether occurring in the ministry of our Lord Jesus Christ or of his disciples or of the apostles. And so they have continued to be, from Antony in the desert to Aelred in Rievaulx, from George Fox to Francis McNutt, and Kathryn Kuhlman to the most timorous teenager in a current prayer group. This of course runs counter to the view that our Lord performed miracles to confirm his messiahship to Israel. It challenges the view that any claim of the Church continuing Christ's ministry of healing today diminishes the glory and greatness of Christ. And it denies the dispensationalism which maintains that the gifts of the Spirit died out in the apostolic age.

The Evidence of Mark

We begin with Mark's gospel. The benefit of being a medical man and not a professional theologian is that, given the time, I can settle in an armchair and read it at a sitting without having to thread a path through the mental traffic of a score of commentaries and a host of introductions. And surely this is how it was meant to be read.

It is usually agreed that Mark was the first gospel to appear. But although an accepted commonplace I have not seen its significance noted – that initially (apart from collections of the sayings of Jesus) there was *only* the gospel of Mark. This gospel, then, was the basic document. We may, if we wish, accept the tradition circulating in the next generation that Mark was guided by Peter, but that is of secondary importance for we believe he was guided by the Holy Spirit. This being so we can take it that Mark's account of our Lord and his ministry was adequate and appropriate as the 'standard life' of Christ; appropriate, that is, to hand to enquirers and to the converts crowding into the churches. If Mark was on the wrong track or even merely giving an incorrect emphasis, then the Church got off on the wrong foot. Of course the gospel was circulating in churches which were also receiving oral teaching from apostles and disciples, therefore it did not need to provide a total picture. Exactly the same situation has existed in twentieth-century mission fields, where Mark has almost always been the first portion of Scripture to be translated and supplied to new converts. The corollary is as true today as in the first century; the teaching it gives must be relevant. We may therefore dismiss the view that our Lord's teaching of the kingdom is inappropriate for the Church age, and that his promises do not apply today.

For my purpose there are four main things that stand out in Mark.

1. The whole thrust is Jesus' proclamation of the kingdom of God. In the course of this proclamation miraculous healings occur as by-products. The very first miracle, an exorcism, occurred unsought when his preaching caused a demoniac to interrupt (1:23). If healing had been his main aim he obviously achieved it when he was mobbed by the sick one evening. Clearly the word was getting around, and without doubt the midnight hills must have been dotted with swift messengers going to sick relatives in distant villages: 'Wake up, get out of bed and we'll somehow get you to Capernaum. Everyone is being healed by a prophet there.' And so they came. Next morning the disciples reported to the Lord: 'They are all looking for you.' We would have expected him to be delighted that here was scope for his healing ministry – if that had been his ministry. But it was not. What he replied was: 'Let's go somewhere else, to the nearby villages, so that I can preach there also' (1:38). A few days later it was while 'he was preaching the word to them' that four men queue-jumped and let their paralysed friend down through the roof

to the feet of Jesus. Seeing their faith Jesus said to the paralysed man: 'My son your sins are forgiven', confirming that
his overruling concern was for the patient's relationship with
God – although simultaneously healing occurred as a by-
product. When he sent out the twelve disciples (3:14) it was
to proclaim the gospel. Their instruction to cast out devils
provided a practical exhibition that the coming of the
kingdom of God meant the expulsion of rebel agents.

 2. Contrary to the common view Jesus' miracles were not
performed to demonstrate his status or divinity (in that age
miracle-workers were not thin on the ground),[5] the very
opposite proves to be the case. The first demoniac heckler
who was proclaiming Jesus as 'the Holy One of God' (1:24)
was ordered to be silent (1:34). The spectator response to this
miracle was 'What is this? A new kind of teaching'. To us
the obvious and desirable question would have been 'Who is
this?' In fact he headed off that question, and later that night
'he would not let the devils speak because they knew who he
was' (1:34 NIV). Surely his disciples were not so clueless that,
had the miracles been intended to raise the question of his
identity, they would have missed the hints. However it is not
until he stills the storm (4:41) that they get around to asking
each other: 'Who can this be?' Now that they have at last
woken up we might naturally expect him to build on that
basis and start using healings to point to his messiahship.
But no. A deaf and dumb man was brought to him. A medical
chief would tell all his students and juniors to gather round
and watch. Not Jesus. He

> took the man aside, away from the crowd, put his fingers
> into his ears, spat, and touched his tongue. Then, looking
> up to heaven, he sighed, and said to him. . . 'Be opened'.
> With that his ears were opened, and at the same time
> the impediment was removed and he spoke plainly. Jesus
> forbade them to tell anyone. (7:33–6 NEB)

Similarly when he healed a blind man he led him out of his
village first, and after healing him sent him home saying: 'Do
not tell anyone in the village' (8:26 NEB). This sounds a futile

instruction as even if he said nothing his newly acquired sight would be obvious within hours. Presumably it was those hours Jesus needed to get away on his preaching mission to the next village, before the mob prevented him.

3. In the first address to the Gentiles, in Cornelius' home (Acts 10:34–43 NEB), Peter said: 'You know about Jesus of Nazareth, how God anointed him with the Holy Spirit and with power. He went about doing good and healing all who were oppressed by the devil, for God was with him.' Mark is shot through with this emphasis on the Holy Spirit in the life of the Lord. In *Jesus and the Spirit* James Dunn[6] indexes 190 Markan passages. We have confirmation of the source of Jesus' power in his confrontation with the doctors of the law; when they claimed of him: 'He is possessed by Beelzebub. . . He drives out devils by the prince of devils' (3:22 NEB), Jesus does not counter by raising the question of his personal status, he rounds on them because they are slandering the Holy Spirit.

4. We have the incredible promises in the latter part of Mark 16. This is not the place to discuss the critical problems of this ending, and there is no need to demand that it is a Markan autograph, but I do not see how we can maintain any serious view of inspiration on the one hand, and on the other allow that these unequivocal promises are spurious, uninspired, and not to be trusted. Christ promised:

> These signs will accompany those who believe: In my name they will drive out demons; they will speak in new tongues; they will pick up snakes with their hands; and when they drink deadly poison, it will not hurt them at all; they will place their hands on sick persons, and they will get well. (16:17–18 NIV)

These are quoted, in this foundation gospel, as the final words of our Lord. Surely they are of no little importance. They have often been taken at their face value, as they were in the following case.

CASE RECORD 6.1

A general practitioner, known to me personally for ten years, reports: At the age of 15, while residing in Taiwan, I contracted viral hepatitis. Because hospital facilities at that time [1965] were rather inadequate where we were, my father, a doctor, decided to look after me at home. Urine and blood tests were taken to confirm the diagnosis which anyway became obvious by the alarming colour of my complexion and massively enlarged liver.

Within two days I had deteriorated so dramatically through persistent vomiting that my father had to put in an intra-venous drip so as to attempt to provide me with some nutriment. Three days after this my mother and a friend of hers from their church came into the room where I was, to pray for me. Having read the passage in the Bible that says 'they shall lay their hands on the sick, and they shall recover' (Mark 16:18 av) they followed this biblical example and prayed for me with the laying on of hands.

I felt nothing, but immediately went to sleep and had a quiet night. When I awoke in the morning the jaundice had entirely gone. The vomiting did not return. I was weak but ravenously hungry. Within 2–3 days I was back, actively on my feet, and raring to go.

It has been impossible for me to believe that the power of God does not heal. In fact, this very belief has led me on many occasions to pray for my own patients and to see a number of situations where the healing has been even more dramatic than in the personal situation I have described.

So much for Mark. Once any historical record is published there are inevitably, and rightly, many who wish to expand it from their own experience. The Burma War volumes on my shelves have my pencilled marginalia. Many readers will recall their own case histories alongside mine. Nowadays many publications may be printed in different editions for different areas. It was so in the first century. Having the gospel (Mark) before them others set about reproducing it in a format suitable for their particular 'market'.

Matthew's Version

Matthew produced his edition for the benefit of the Jewish community. Hence the frequent linkage of events in the life of Jesus with Old Testament prophecy by use of the recurring phrase: 'This was to fulfil the words of the prophet.' (The most important of these quotes for our study, that from Isaiah 53, is discussed in Chapter 8.) Despite this, and the use of 'sacrifice' as a portmanteau word for all the Old Testament regulations, it is Matthew who notes on two occasions (9:13 and 12:7) – as the Gentile gospels do not – that our Lord quotes the text, 'I will have mercy and not sacrifice'.

The temptation in the wilderness. While Mark mentions Jesus' temptation in the wilderness in two sentences (1:12–13), Matthew expands to give us details (4:1–11). Of the many angles from which this episode can be studied, the following seems germane to my thesis. Satan knew perfectly well who Jesus was, therefore there was no question of his yielding to the temptation to worship him. There was presumably also some danger to the tempter as more than twelve legions of angels (26:53) were on red alert. What purpose motivated him to take the risk? This at any rate: to tempt our Lord to 'pull rank'. If Jesus could be persuaded, even once, to use his divine power or authority or status in a terrestrial situation, then he would have put himself out of our league. Any later suggestion or command that we should follow in his steps, do similar works, heal, or exorcise, would be unreasonable, in fact ludicrous. Whereas Matthew prefaces this account with the information that it was the Spirit who set up this encounter (4:1), Luke concludes his parallel account (4:14) with 'Then Jesus, armed with the power of the Spirit, returned to Galilee' (NEB).

It is in Matthew that we get further evidence that our Lord

did not consider miracles to be unique proof of status, for in discussing the day of judgment he tells of some who will be dismissed from his presence even although they could claim in his name to have prophesied, cast out demons and done many miracles (7:21–3).

Matthew summarises: 'So Jesus went round all the towns and villages teaching in their synagogues, announcing the good news of the Kingdom, and curing every kind of ailment and disease. The sight of the people moved him to pity: they were like sheep without a shepherd, harrassed and helpless' (9:35–6 NEB). The primacy of kingdom proclamation is as clear here as it is in Mark.

My argument so far is buttoned up in our Lord's words to the Pharisees, omitted by Mark but recorded by Matthew (12:28) 'If it is by the Spirit of God that I drive out the devils, then be sure the kingdom of God has already come upon you' (NEB).

In Matthew's selection of healing miracles there is from the start an emphasis on the acknowledging, by the needy, of the power at Jesus' command. He begins with the leprosy patient's challenge: ' "Sir, if only you will, you can cleanse me." Jesus stretched out his hand, touched him, and said, "Indeed I will; be clean again" ' (8:1–3 NEB); and follows this with the centurion's astounding statement, 'You need only say the word and the boy will be cured' (8:8 NEB). The same emphasis is seen in one of the two cures only recorded by Matthew. The two blind men who called out to Jesus are challenged by him: 'Do you believe that I have the power to do what you want?' (9:28 NEB).

In other words he is looking for faith. That element is listed in seven of the miracles recorded by Matthew. Faith in the power, the authority, which is available to Jesus. 'The people were filled with awe at the sight, and praised God for granting such authority to men' (9:8 NEB). And it is a power and authority he shares with his disciples: 'he called his twelve disciples to him and gave them authority to cast out unclean spirits and to cure every kind of ailment and disease' (10:1 NEB).

After recounting Christ's passion Matthew returns to this theme and this commission in the climax and culmination of his gospel; in the words of the risen Lord:

Full authority in heaven and earth has been committed to me. Go, therefore, make disciples of all the nations; baptise them in the name of the Father and the Son and the Holy Spirit, and teach them to observe all the commands I gave you. And know that I am with you always; yes, to the end of time" (28:19–20).

Luke's Histories

Luke's history: his gospel and the Acts; written by a physician who aims to present a chronological account, is especially congenial to our patterns of thought. The details of Mary's pregnancy can only have come from her own lips; women feel freer to talk about such matters to members of the medical profession. There are other professional touches; Luke alone notes that Peter's mother-in-law's fever was high (4:38); and whereas the other versions talk of a leper coming to Jesus, to Luke he was an advanced case (5:12). Mark and Matthew tell us of the healing of the man with a withered hand; Luke notes that it was his right hand (6:6). Whereas Mark, the layman, writing of the woman with menorrhagia records she 'had suffered much under many physicians, and had spent all that she had, and was no better but rather grew worse' (5:26), Luke, understanding the limitations of medicine, writes: 'Among them was a woman who had suffered from haemorrhages for twelve years; and nobody had been able to cure her' (8:43 NEB). Our hearts warm to him. It is Luke who records that Jesus explained to this gynaecological patient the mode of her healing: 'I felt that power had gone out from me' (8:46 NEB); and in an earlier passage (6:19) that 'everyone in the crowd was trying to touch him, because power went out from him and cured them all' (NEB).

Preeminently it is Luke who emphasises the source of Jesus'

119

power: the Holy Spirit. God the Holy Spirit is mentioned at the beginning of the gospel in Gabriel's promise about John the Baptist. He is the inspiration of the prophetic utterances of Elizabeth (1:42), Zechariah (1:67) and Simeon (2:26). To Mary, Gabriel announces that the Holy Spirit will be the agent for her divine *in-vivo* fertilisation (1:35). The Holy Spirit descended on Jesus at his baptism in the Jordan (3:22) and then: 'Full of the Holy Spirit, Jesus returned from the Jordan, and for forty days was led by the Spirit up and down the wilderness and tempted by the devil' (4:1–2 NEB). 'Then Jesus, armed with the power of the Spirit, returned to Galilee' (4:14 NEB), to astonish the members of his synagogue in Nazareth by announcing:

> The Spirit of the Lord is upon me because he has anointed me; he has sent me to announce good news to the poor, to proclaim release for prisoners and recovery of sight for the blind; to let the broken victims go free, to proclaim the year of the Lord's favour. (4:18–19 NEB)

Recording that crowds from every village in Galilee, and from Judaea and Jerusalem, flocked to Jesus, Luke emphasises the same point: 'the power of the Lord was with him to heal the sick' (5:17 NEB). The question I have not seen anyone addressing is this: if our Lord Jesus in his earthly ministry employed his own powers as the Second Person of the Trinity, why did he need the Third Person? In these circumstances what could the Holy Spirit do/give which our Lord Jesus could not do in his own power? However it is clear from the many passages I have quoted that in fact Jesus did rely on the Holy Spirit's power throughout his life on this planet.

This power he did not keep to himself: after all, had not the herald John the Baptist announced: 'He will baptise you with the Holy Spirit and with fire' (3:16 NIV)? So 'he called the Twelve together and gave them power and authority to overcome all the devils and to cure diseases, and sent them to proclaim the kingdom of God and to heal' (9:1–2 NEB).

The feeding of the five thousand. That mission triumphantly fulfilled, the disciples return to the situation where five thousand or more around Jesus are about to be benighted. They suggest that he sends the crowd away to find food and shelter. His reply is staggering. 'You give them something to eat' (9:13 NIV). And in view of their recent experiences, why not? But they shirk the challenge. So Jesus has to give them a further tutorial. To understand this we turn to John's description of the incident (6:1–13); or rather to the happenings of the next day when boat-loads of people came ashore near the site of the feeding of the five thousand. But John does not use that obvious identification. What he writes is: 'Boats from Tiberias, however, came ashore near the place where the people had eaten the bread over which the Lord gave thanks' (6:23 NEB). To return to Luke: when the disciples baulked at dealing with the problem Jesus got them to seat the people. That is the promise, you will not be left hungry. Then taking the five loaves and the two fishes and looking up to heaven, he gave thanks and broke them. Having taught them that lesson, he handed the miracle back to the disciples, and the boy's picnic is multiplied in their hands as it is set before the people (9:16). It is the technique all of us use in teaching our juniors; 'All right, I'll do this tricky bit. OK now? Right, you take over again.' John's surprising choice of phrase for the location proves that the disciples got the message.

It is a common mistake to imagine that these special powers were given to the inner circle of the twelve. It was not so. Shortly afterwards we read that our Lord commissioned an additional seventy-two: 'Heal the sick who are there and tell them, "The kingdom of God is near you" ' (10:9 NIV). Returning jubilant our Lord encouraged them: 'I watched how Satan fell, like lightning, out of the sky. And now you see that I have given you the power to tread underfoot snakes and scorpions and all the forces of the enemy, and nothing will ever harm you' (10:17–19 NEB). If this power, this promise, was for the next few months only, then our Lord's choice of that last phrase was, to say the least, inept, and Luke must have felt very embarrassed quoting it years later. It is the promise with which Mark's gospel ended. However

Luke in his edition decided to emphasise the motive power of the whole enterprise by concluding with Christ's final promise: 'And mark this: I am sending upon you my Father's promised gift; so stay here in this city until you are armed with the power from above' (24:49 NEB). That arming with power is to be described in the account of Pentecost early in Luke's second book (Acts 2).

I set out to defend my thesis that all Jesus' miracles were done in the power of God the Holy Spirit. I was possibly too cautious. He never stopped relying on the Holy Spirit. We have noted Luke emphasising this by ending his gospel with Christ's promise on the day of his ascension. He returns to that occasion at the beginning of Acts and hammers it home with this astonishing phrase: 'I wrote of all that Jesus did and taught from the beginning until the day when, after giving instructions *through the Holy Spirit* to the apostles whom he had chosen, he was taken up to heaven' (1:1–2 NEB). My case rests.

John's Gospel

Our Lord in his talk with the disciples on the night before his passion promised that 'the Counsellor, the Holy Spirit, whom the father will send in my name, will teach you all things and will remind you of everything I have said to you'. John, who records this (14:26 NIV) had experienced it as he meditated throughout his lifetime. So he wrote a completely new work. This is the advanced book in which a knowledge of the basic text is taken for granted: for instance none of the twenty-two accounts of healing in the synoptic gospels is repeated by John. He makes his purpose clear in writing: 'Jesus did many other miraculous signs in the presence of his disciples, which are not recorded in this book. But these are written that you may believe that Jesus is the Christ, the Son of God, and that by believing you may have life in his name' (20:30–1 NIV). Every single thing recorded by John is directed to building up a picture of who Jesus was, and recording reactions as this unfolded.

Having boldly started by naming our Lord as the Word (1:1), he reports John the Baptist announcing Jesus as the Lamb (1:29), the baptiser with the Holy Spirit (1:33); Andrew's naming him the Messiah (1:41); Phillip as the one spoken of by Moses and the prophets (1:45); Nathaniel's avowal, 'You are the Son of God, the King of Israel' (1:49); and on through more than thirty statements, to Thomas's 'My Lord and my God' (20:28). Every section of the work is directed either to a further revelation by our Lord of his nature, or to its discovery by the crowds; with their recurrent debates, and attempts to arrest or stone him as the implications of his claims dawned.

The four miracles of healing John gives are inserted as part of this undeviating theme. After concluding his account of the turning of water into wine (not a healing miracle) with, 'This deed at Cana-in-Galilee is the first of the signs by which Jesus revealed his glory and led his disciples to believe in him (2:11 NEB); he then records the official's son being healed at Cana as the second of the signs (4:54).

John immediately goes on to the healing of the paralysed man by the Sheep-Pool on the Sabbath, to climax it with:

> It was works of this kind done on the Sabbath that stirred the Jews to persecute Jesus. He defended himself by saying, 'My Father has never ceased his work, and I am working too.' This made the Jews still more determined to kill him, because he was not only breaking the Sabbath, but, by calling God his own Father, he claimed equality with God. (5:16–18 NEB)

In the third healing, that of the man congenitally blind, John's technique and aim is clear. It is exactly like a demonstration in the undergraduate clinical medical class: the actual healing is disposed of in two verses (9:6–7) without any reference to the patient's feelings.

His disciples asked him, 'Rabbi, who sinned, this man or

123

his parents, that he was born blind?' 'Neither this man nor his parents sinned,' said Jesus, 'but this happened so that the work of God might be displayed in his life. . . While I am in the world I am the light of the world.' (9:2–5 NIV)

Then John launches into thirty verses of follow-up in which the patient's understanding of the person of Jesus is forced upwards, largely by the negative reactions of the Pharisees. Even his parents realise that this is the crux of the issue, and back away (9:22–3). The patient, having started with the bald estimate, 'He is a prophet' (9:17), is nettled by the questioners, who are getting on his back, into exploding:

What an extraordinary thing! Here is a man who has opened my eyes, yet you do not know where he comes from! . . . To open the eyes of a man born blind – it is unheard of since time began. If that man had not come from God he could have done nothing. (9:30–3 NEB)

So he is expelled from the synagogue, and Jesus, learning this, found him. ' " Have you faith in the Son of Man?" The man answered, "Tell me who he is, sir, that I should put my faith in him." "You have seen him," said Jesus; "indeed, it is he who is speaking to you." "Lord, I believe" ' (9:35–8 NEB). John has been able to build up his argument another stage.

He uses the identical technique in his fourth healing story, the raising of Lazarus. In passing, it says something of the mass of material at their disposal that none of the other gospellers (and Matthew, at any rate, was almost certainly present) got round to recording this event. News of Lazarus' illness elicits Jesus' statement: 'This illness will not end in death; it has come for the glory of God, to bring glory to the Son of God' (11:4 NEB). As that is the aim there has got to be time for the situation to develop. 'And therefore, though he loved Martha and her sister and Lazarus, after hearing of his illness Jesus waited for two days in the place where he was' (11:5–6 NEB). We then read his talk with Martha leading up to a new revelation of our Lord in his assertion: ('I am the resurrection and I am life', and Martha's response, 'I now believe that you are the Messiah, the Son of God, who was to come into the world' (11:25, 27 NEB). Lazarus is then raised, which leads to the High Priest's prophecy that Jesus would die for the nation; and John thus ends the pericope with: 'would die not for the nation alone but to gather together the scattered children of God' (11:50–2 NEB).

It may seem that John's gospel, with its single-minded purpose of elucidating the nature of Jesus, is unimportant for our study. That is far from the case for he records our Lord's talk with his disciples on the evening before his passion. Early in the discourse he made the bold statement that his words and works were not in his own strength or authority: 'it is the Father, living in me, who is doing this work' (14:10 NIV). He then adds: 'I tell you most solemnly, whoever believes in me will perform the same works as I do myself, he will perform even greater works, because I am going to the Father' (14:12 JB). How? 'I shall ask the Father, and he will give you another Advocate, to be with you forever . . . it is for your good that I am leaving you. If I do not go, your Advocate will not come' (14:16 JB; 16:7 NEB).

John probably wrote those words half a century or more after the ascension. Did he write as a mere historian: 'that's what Jesus said, pity it never came off'; or wistfully: 'it was great in that springtime, tragic that the hopes faded'. We must ask ourselves again: does John write as though Christ's promises had proved hollow, his assurances unfounded?

The Acts of the Apostles

We have no need to speculate: in the Acts of the Apostles we can read the reality of the early experiences of the disciples. Those disciples, who forty-eight hours after listening to Jesus' promises were cowering in fear behind locked doors, were to turn the world upside down (17:6). There is no time here to follow their experience of the Holy Spirit filling and again and further filling them (2:4; 4:8, 31). While they realised that it was God the Holy Spirit in the Old Testament days who had been the instructor of David (4:25) and of Isaiah (28:25), now they were experiencing him constantly in everyday life. It was the Holy Spirit who witnessed alongside them (5:32). It was he, when the convoy of Ethiopian carriages came along, who gave practical instructions as to which one Philip was to hitch a lift in (8:29), and later translocated him elsewhere (8:39). The Holy Spirit it was who interrupted Peter's first sermon to the Gentiles (10:45) having earlier broken down his reluctance. He gave specific verbal orders to the church at Antioch (13:2), and made his will so clear to a committee that its chairman could write: 'It is the decision of the Holy Spirit, and our decision. . .' (15:28). Paul's sensible plans had to be altered, not once but twice, on the Holy Spirit's orders (16:6–8).

Throughout the Acts we find the Holy Spirit working in this way, making specific facts known. It is clear that only such Spirit-imparted knowledge could have made Peter act so incisively in the affair of Ananias and Sapphira (5:1–10). The Spirit constrained Paul to go to Jerusalem but gave detailed information of the problems that would face him (20:22–3). While he was at Caesarea the prophet Agabus 'took Paul's belt, bound his own feet and hands with it, and said, "These are the words of the Holy Spirit: Thus will the Jews in Jerusalem bind the man to whom this belt belongs, and hand him over to the Gentiles" ' (21:11 NEB).

Today we find him active in just the same way, imparting 'words of knowledge'. His activity can be illustrated in the following case, where the treatment was medically orthodox but diagnosis was the direct activity of the Holy Spirit. The vision has been confirmed to me by the medical practitioner who was one of the elders present, and was recorded in the patient's letter to me, received before I first saw her in my clinic in 1984. This letter is filed in her NHS case notes.

CASE RECORD 6.2

This patient had had an abdominal hysterectomy performed at the age of twenty-nine. Eighteen months later she was in a psychiatric hospital under treatment for depression, and while there was seen by a local gynaecologist for her complaint of constant pain.

On returning home she was referred, with the same complaint, back to Sunderland, where her original operation had been performed. Before this appointment she asked for prayer from the elders of her church. They came to her house bringing with them one of the church members who has a particular gift in this field of healing. This lady, while the patient was being prayed for and anointed with oil, had a vision from the Lord that something she could only describe as 'a sort of internal tuck' was causing the problem.

The patient was plucking up her courage to tell the consultant this, as she felt he would be sympathetic, but was in fact seen by the senior registrar, and her courage failed her. He admitted her for examination under anaesthesia, but found nothing amiss and discharged her. She felt the Lord had let her down.

A month later my colleague received a letter from the patient's GP. 'She is complaining bitterly of the pain, and crying like anything. I am afraid she is heading for another nervous breakdown right now because of the pain. I would be grateful if you would see her personally.' This letter was initialled by the consultant and sent down to appointments office for a date. By an inexplicable 'clerical error' (for his name was written clearly on the form), the appointment was made for my clinic. Before coming she wrote and told me the story.

At the out-patients visit my findings were not very definite; in fact I drew a diagram with the suggestion of a vague swelling on the right side. However in view of this story I arranged to admit her and look inside her abdomen by laparoscope. The operation notes record: 'massive band of adhesions between bowels and lateral pelvic wall, burying left ovary'. I dealt with these problems, which, it will be noted, were not what I had expected from my out-patients findings, but were what the Spirit had revealed to the praying group in the patient's home.

Two months later I received another letter from the patient:

'I explained to you my fears regarding the mental aspect as I had previously been told that the pain was all in my mind. Because of this I had vowed I would never voluntarily tell anyone about my previous mental history – How the Lord works to release us! I am now feeling marvellous – better than I have ever felt in the last five years, and on Sunday last agreed to testify to the way in which the Lord brought about my healing.

'As I spoke, I found the Lord prompting me to spill out all the old fears and anxieties as a way of really bringing home what he had done for me, and even as I spoke, I felt a real cleansing out and healing of my mind even in that instant. . .'

(At the present time of writing her pastor has volunteered to me the news that she is well and happy and that her witness for the Lord is strong.)

Our interest however is principally in the healing miracles performed by the apostles. There is a fascinating facet of the first one, the healing of the congenital cripple: we learn that he used to be carried every day and set down to beg at the Beautiful Gate of the temple. This had obviously been going on for a long time, for he was now forty and we are told that after his cure everyone recognised him as the beggar (3:1–16; 4:21–2). But only two months previously our Lord had been going in and out of the temple and must very often have passed this man. It is hard to avoid the conclusion that whenever he went past he said to himself, 'I'm leaving that one for my disciples.' The healings in the gospels and those in the Acts are a continuum.

We can count seventeen separate miraculous cures in the Acts, but if we are trying to quantify this activity the figure is meaningless. Almost at the beginning (5:12) we read: 'many remarkable and wonderful things took place among the people at the hands of the apostles' (NEB); and a little later, Stephen 'began to work great miracles and signs' (6:8), as did Philip (8:6, 13) and Paul and Barnabas (14:3). Even Peter's shadow (5:15) and Paul's clothing (19:12) were curative. We are talking of a very large number of people cured, and not only by the leading figures – of those I have named only Peter was of the twelve apostles – the activity is common to the whole company.

The geographical scope of the Holy Spirit's healings now far exceeded the circumscribed limits of Jesus' ministry, for it reached Ephesus in Asia Minor (19:12), Phillipi in Greece (16:18), and Malta (28:8–9). The spectacular quality of his work did not diminish: even the dead were still raised (9:40; 20:10).

But what happened after that first generation? That is the question we must investigate in the next chapter.

1. H. H. Henson, *Notes on Spiritual Healing* (London, Williams & Norgate 1925), p. 120.
2. C. Brown, *Miracles and the Critical Mind*. Exeter, Paternoster; and Grand Rapids, W. B. Eerdmans 1984.
3. J. S. Baxter, *Divine Healing of the Body*. Zondervan 1979.
4. *Bede's Ecclesiastical History of the English People*, ed. B. Colgrave and R. A. B. Mynors (Oxford, Clarendon Press 1969), III.5.
5. H. C. Kee, *Miracle in the Early Christian World: a study in sociohistorical method*. New Haven and London, Yale 1983.
6. J. D. G. Dunn, *Jesus and the Spirit*. London, SCM 1975.

7

Miracles:
temporary phenomena or permanent gift?

The Function of Miracles

We saw in Chapter 4 that miracles have continued throughout the Christian age. The question is, were these a disconnected series of answers to prayer, 'unconvenanted mercies'? To pinpoint the issue by crude analogy, has God the Father doled them out like a headmaster granting an unexpected half-holiday, or perhaps as a Victorian lady in a particularly hard winter handing out provisions to her needy retainers? Or is there some better explanation, some deeper pattern?

It would be useful to begin by asking how we are to understand the New Testament miracles. Were they like a first-stage rocket, designed to fall away when the Church was safely in orbit? When in America, we saw the John F. Kennedy spaceport and were astonished at the gigantic size, and yet expendability, of the rockets required to put the vital capsule into orbit. Is that the picture: dramatic, immensely powerful, but necessary only for blast-off? Or are they an integral part – the power-unit in fact – of the life of the Church? A few days earlier we had been in the swamps at the headwaters of the Suwannee river, exploring the waterways in a small boat with an outboard motor. The only living things in sight were alligators' heads. While we were unlikely to sink, we were keenly aware that everything depended on the constant functioning of that motor. Is that a more appropriate picture?

Miraculous healings are only one of the charismata – the gifts of the Spirit – among which we have not been offered an option. It is astonishing how many of us act as though we have hit the coconut at the fair and been offered the choice of one reward. We are happy to accept healing and shun the other gifts. No, the question is, was this package of gifts for then only or for always?

The Continuity of the Charismata

As Christians down the centuries have looked at the state of the Church in their own day, and found it woefully inadequate compared with the life of the Church in the first century, they have had two options. They could admit their present experience to be deficient, therefore culpable; in other words there was something wrong. But as such an admission would be pretty traumatic it has rarely been allowed to surface into consciousness. The alternative choice was to maintain that God had changed the rules, the power-loss was not their fault but due to his withdrawing it. This easier option is the one almost universally grasped. By the time the options were out in the open and had to be faced centuries had gone by. Theology has moulded itself to the current situation, rather as, when a pregnant woman loses her waters too soon, the womb will mould itself round the baby in a 'hug-me-tight' uterus: a highly worrying state for the obstetrician. This hug-me-tight theology has been developed by generations of devout scholarly men; we have got used to it, it is comfortable. We have rightly been defending a package of beliefs against a multitude of foes: how ridiculous and foolish it seems now to admit that it may be inadequate. Better not rock the boat!

I have been visiting 'my' quads in their incubators in the regional intensive care baby unit. Once their vital functions are safely working it will be possible to withdraw their external support systems and they will be removed from the incubators. In a few weeks I will let their parents take them home, and they will no longer need such special care; although other help has been arranged. Such was the view which held the field almost unchallenged for fourteen centuries, that the gifts (or at any rate the more spectacular

131

gifts) of the Spirit were withdrawn once the Church was safely established.

We may take the writings of B. B. Warfield as typifying this position, and because he has been so influential we must spend some time looking at them. His thesis propounded in the opening pages of *Counterfeit Miracles*[1] is that the apostolic Church was a miracle-working church, so that 'the exception would be, not a church with, but a church without, such gifts'. However this was:

> the characterizing peculiarity of specifically the Apostolic Church, and it *belonged therefore exclusively* to the Apostolic age. . . These gifts were not the possession of the primitive Christian as such, nor for that matter of the Apostolic Church or the Apostolic age for themselves; they were distinctively the authentication of the Apostles. They were part of the credentials of the Apostles as the authoritative agents of God in founding the church. Their functions *thus confined them to distinctively the Apostolic church, and they necessarily passed away with it.* (my italics)

Warfield is at pains to deny that the charismata were to support the Church, they were authentications of the apostles; symbols of status, badges of rank, commissions. Unfashionable though these things are nowadays, we should not discard this idea out of hand. I once moderated a meeting of the Uganda Kirk Session when only half a dozen elders were present. We gathered at the home of one of them. The acting session clerk swept up the drive in his beflagged Rolls Royce without number plates, with an escort of police motor-cyclists. As Governor-General representing the Queen his status had to be displayed at all times because it reflected hers. This appears to be rather how Warfield saw the apostles. It was also a view held in the seventeenth century by Mennonites, Seekers, and Quakers.[2] Of their forerunners we are told that they awaited a man with apostolic power proved by the signs and evidences by which the original apostles established their claims to leadership, namely the performance of miracles.

Despite his denial Warfield's view proves to be the

'temporary support for the infant church' one, for what other function was there for these apostolic powers but to build up the Church in its initial stages?

There is however a more important flaw in his argument. He has misunderstood the function of the Holy Spirit's gifts. They are not given as decorations to be worn as symbols of authority even although they would be exercised only for the benefit of others. They are gifts to the body of Christ for everyday use (1 Cor. 12:4–30; 14:12, 26) for the good of that body, whether in its local or its universal manifestation. The person who has been granted them, whether for a particular task or more long-term, does not merit any kudos. Saul of Tarsus did not receive his sight back at the hands of one of the apostles but at those of Ananias of Damascus, who is never mentioned before or afterwards in the biblical record. We can paraphrase Warfield's footnote[3] on this case as: 'Ah, but the difference is that while Ananias could perform a miracle, the apostles – and they only – had the power to impart the gift of working miracles to those on whom they laid their hands.' If he is right then the gifts could exist only for one further generation, but no more.

I cannot believe that people who hold those views have ever sat down and considered what this would have involved in the late first century. Let us picture the scene they imply. Over there is church A, which, having been visited recently by one of the few surviving apostles, has its many members demonstrating the different gifts. Beyond in the next valley is church B, which he did not have time to visit and as a result has no gifted members left, and inevitably sees itself as second-rate, having to organise regular convoys of sick over the mountain to A, which is manifestly in a different spiritual class altogether. Church C was similarly barren until a teenage lass blessed with gifts moved there from church A on marriage. She can minister her gifts but cannot impart that ability to anyone else. Would that scenario really fulfil the promise and picture we read about in the gospels? As John looked out of his window, choosing the next words for the gospel he was writing, is that the scene he saw? And if it was,

can anyone seriously believe he would have dared to write
what he did?

The Witness of the Apostolic Fathers

Warfield sets out to support his views with a discussion of
early church history; but we do not need to consider his
arguments as they have been overtaken, and overturned, by
Evelyn Frost's doctoral study, *Christian Healing: a consideration
of the place of spiritual healing in the Church of today in the light of
the doctrine and practice of the ante-Nicene Church*.[4] Following her
guidance we can look at each post-apostolic generation.

Justin Martyr wrote to the Senate around AD 150 'of the
many Christian men in your city who . . . have healed and
do heal, rendering helpless and driving the possessing devils
out of the men though they could not be cured by all the
other exorcists'. That of course does not absolutely prove my
point for they could have received anointing from John, for
we know that one of his disciples, Polycarp, was not martyred
until AD 155.

However a generation later Irenaeus wrote of his fellow-
Christians:

> Others still heal the sick by laying their hands upon them,
> and they are made whole. Yes, moreover, as I have said,
> the dead even have been raised up, and remained among
> us for many years. And what shall I more say? It is not
> possible to name the number of the gifts which the Church,
> scattered throughout the whole world, has received from
> God, in the Name of Jesus Christ . . . and which she exerts
> day by day for the benefit of the gentiles.

Moving on yet another generation Tertullian gave evidence
of the Emperor Severus having been healed by holy anointing
at the hands of the Christian Proculus, who in gratitude for
this was maintained in the imperial palace to the day of his
death. Severus for his part died in Eboracum – our city of
York: if he were to return there today he would find those

same gifts of healing in practice. Tertullian wrote of many other men of rank (as well as humbler folk) being healed and of these facts being verifiable in official sources.

One more generation and we reach Origen who wrote: 'By these means [invocation of the God of all things, and of Jesus along with a mention of his history] we too have seen many people freed from grievous calamities, and from distractions of mind, and madness, and countless other ills, which could not be cured by men nor devils.'

In these quotations, starting in the lifetime of the apostles' disciples, and going on generation by generation, is there the slightest evidence of a great divide, of a great sense of loss? We are fortunate in having English translations of the apostolic Fathers,[5] whose epistles were written in the second century, and also *Eusebius' History of the Church*,[6] written early in the fourth century (and we are doubly fortunate in that they are readily available in popular paperback). These give not a hint of Warfield's cut-off.

Evelyn Frost has pages of quotations from the early Fathers. Some of these writings were addressed to Roman authorities, with the invitation to check up on the statements. And so we come to the time of Augustine, arguably the greatest of all Christian theologians.

Augustine's views. A recent author[7] makes his own attitude clear: 'Were these (Chrysostom and Augustine) and others of their period such spiritual pygmies that the gifts could not be bestowed in their day? Or had the gifts ceased as God intended?' and goes on to write with understandable asperity of those who quote Augustine but fail to provide verifiable references to his writings. As this is a matter of importance we will have to look into it with such care as is possible here, well aware that an adequate study of Augustine would be a lifetime's work.

Augustine, writes Professor Robert Markus[8] 'had a mind always on the move, constantly questioning itself, critical of habitual assumptions, stimulated by the concerns of friends, responding to the ever-changing problems thrown up by controversy with opponents, and later, to the needs of his congregation.' It is therefore not surprising that towards the end of his life he wrote a book called *Retractions*, correcting some of his earlier writings. A convenient summary of his change of view can be found in Morton Kelsey's *Healing and Christianity*.[9] We read that in Augustine's earlier writings he stated specifically that Christians are not to look for continuance of the healing gift. 'Then something happened, his skepticism gave way to belief in Christ's healing power, and he frankly admitted that he had been wrong. . . Nearly forty years after his conversion, when his *City of God* was nearing completion his outlook changed'; as Book 22 of that work amply illustrates. Then Augustine wrote:

> . . . once I realised how many miracles were occurring in our own day . . . and also how wrong it would be to allow the memory of these marvels of divine power to perish from among our people. It is only two years ago that the keeping of records was begun here in Hippo, and already, at this writing, we have nearly seventy attested miracles.

By stepping down to our paperback bookshop we can pick up a copy of Augustine's last work, *The City of God*, and check for ourselves. There, in Book 22, Chapters 8–10,[10] a series of miracles of healing are reported. He starts with the healing of Innocentius, some time counsellor of the vice-prefecture, who was suffering from fistulae (ulcers): 'I was present as an eye-witness. . .'; and ends with the healing of a brother and sister on consecutive days, during services which Augustine was conducting in his own cathedral.

Possidius, his close friend for forty years, wrote his Life of St Augustine[11] a mere two or three years after the latter's death. It is a work highly respected by scholars. He records that during his terminal illness Augustine was visited by someone who brought a sick friend, and asked him to lay his hands on him so that he might recover. He at first demurred on the grounds that he did not have any personal gift of healing:

But the man insisted that he had had a vision and had been told in his dream, 'Go to Bishop Augustine and get him to lay his hands on him and he will recover.' Informed of this, Augustine acted on it without further delay and the Lord at once enabled the sick person to leave his presence healed.

It seems reasonable to sum up Augustine's position when Bishop of Hippo, at the culmination of his life, in his own words:[12] 'I have been concerned that such accounts should be published because I saw that signs of divine power like those of older days were frequently occurring in modern times too. . .'

We have come full circle back to Augustine's contemporary, Martin of Tours, whose gifts we looked at in Chapter 4. But so far in these quotations, starting with the disciples of the apostles and going on generation by generation, we have covered the interval without a gap. Where have we been conscious of a clear-cut divide, a sudden knowledge of loss, a realisation that the promises of the gospels – rather the promises given by our Lord himself – have been withdrawn? Surely if the commonly held argument (as typified by Warfield) was true there would somewhere in the second-century writings have been an even greater cry of loss and dereliction than when the Ark of the Lord was lost to Israel (1 Sam. 4:21): 'Ichabod. . . The glory is departed.'

Raising the Dead: today?

However we have even better grounds for belief that the promises were not withdrawn – our current experiences exemplified in the Case Reports. Despite this there are always those who play what they see to be the trump card: 'If this is so, if those fabulous promises are still true as you say, then where are the cases of raising the dead?'

We have already noted such an incident in the early days of the Scottish Reformation, but to find the like in the second half of our own century is something else. Well, here it is.

137

CASE RECORD 7.1

In 1963 Robin Talbot and his wife, of the Overseas Missionary Fellowship, were the first Christians to reside in the village of Still Water in the Mong tribal area of North Thailand. Mrs Ling, aged about 50, was the first villager to destroy her domestic spirit-shelf and become a Christian. The villagers warned her that ill would come of it. It did. She became sick. While the missionaries prayed with her the villagers gathered round and watched, while the local animist priest jeered. She died. At least in the opinion of the villagers, to whom death is no stranger, and of the missionaries, she died.

Robin Talbot tells me that he felt in a corner. Only God could get him out. Here was a test case like that of Elijah versus the prophets of Baal on Mount Carmel (1 Kings 18:19–39). The missionaries were at the end of the road with no further ideas. 'I had to hand it over to God: "It's in your court"; not without hope, but with no specific guidance as to what would happen.'

After ten minutes he heard Mrs Ling speaking quietly and calmly. Her eighteen-year-old son grabbed her and shouted, 'Who are you talking to? Where are you?' As they listened they discovered they were hearing her half of her conversation with Jesus who was walking along with her. At one stage she got frightened and agitated near a pit when demons tried to grab her. But, as she explained later, Jesus got hold of her hand.

She sat up. She called out to the villagers individually by name and revealed a knowledge of their previously unknown secrets. So accurate and devastating were these that the village priest's son fled, to return half an hour later and announce that he wished to become a Christian. (He is now elder of the church.)

Mrs Ling reported that she had met Christ, had seen in heaven, but had been told that she must go back and report what she had seen. Though she had never attended any sort of church service and could not read, she now gave proof of being a deeply instructed Christian. She later learned to read in one month, instead of the expected six.

There are of course no EEG records, no medically satisfying proof that she ever died – even if medicine was in fact fully agreed on the definition of death. However her sudden acquisition of knowledge is inexplicable without recourse to divine intervention. But, accepting that she died, this resurrection is purely a work of God, almost beyond hope, and not claimed specifically in prayer by the Christians present. Can we get a better example of raising the dead: prayed for and happening? We can.

The following Chilean case, which occurred in the late 1970s, is quoted verbatim from a letter I received from Miss Kath Clark of the (Anglican) South American Missionary Society.

CASE RECORD 7.2

The case that I know of resurrection from the dead took place in the country district near Salta Pura, which is several kilometres from Nueva Imperial in the ninth region. It was when Andres Montupil, a Mapuche evangelist, had been commissioned to do evangelistic work in an area where there was no church. He spent the whole day, as far as I remember, in a series of visits to this very hard area. He had spent the whole day with no success at all. He had had drink thrown over him by those who were quaffing and scoffing. One threw out the remark, 'If you want to do anything with your message, there's someone who needs you over yonder,' pointing in the inimitable way they do with their chin.

And it transpired that there was a child, 13 or 14 years old, who was very ill. And so Andres found his way to the haystack-like house which was the 'ruta' where they lived, and he knew immediately that he had come to the right one because the howling of uncontrollable grief and hope-

139

lessness could be heard outside, and he knew it was a Mapuche woman grieving at the time of death.

I understand that Andres drew near the house praying very much and went in and comforted the woman in the usual way of a hug and giving the 'besame' – saying the approved words, 'I feel with you.' He was able very gently to lead her outside the house to where there was a clear view of the cordillera (the mountains), and was able to say, 'My Father made this, and your Father too, and he has power to raise up your daughter who is dead, and we are going to pray.' He returned to the house. The child was still lying on the bed where she had just died. Everyone was distraught. She was by now cold and stiffening. Andres took off his coat to get down to prayer and he said, 'We all prayed and nothing happened, and the second time we all prayed again and nothing happened.'

And he said the third time: 'Lord, for your glory, so the people know you exist and that you have power, raise their daughter.' And the third time she coughed, moved, and there was life.

Andres was able to call for something to be given to eat, some thin soup, and he stayed in the home for two or three days teaching them about the Lord. Neighbours came in because they had heard of the death and some came for the wake, and found the child awake. The family came to know the Lord, and a church was formed.

[Miss Clark concludes:] I subsequently met the girl and the family and the church.

The evidence of death in this case is better than in our Thailand case. There had been time for the bereaved parents to send out to friends to tell them, and the corpse was stiffening. And here we have a Christian specifically praying for the raising of the dead – going out on a limb telling the bereaved mother that his God could do it.

In view of all this evidence there is no way, no way at all, in which we can accept the theory that his gifts (or at least the miraculous gifts) were withdrawn by God the Holy Spirit after the death of the first two generations of Christians. There is not the slightest biblical teaching that it would be so, there is not the slightest historical evidence in contemporary records that it was so, and there is abundant contemporary evidence that they continued; and still continue. I submit that that 'withdrawn' viewpoint must now be abandoned, once and for all.

There is a more widely held view that the gifts disappeared at some later date up to the 'conversion' of the Roman Empire early in the fourth century. Theoretically it would be possible to hold this view and yet concede that miracles were reappearing in our own day. However it cannot be sustained in the light of the cases I have quoted from the history of the Church in the intervening centuries. We noted in the Thailand incident (Case Record 7.1) that the heathen prophesied that ill would come of an abandonment of the old beliefs, and jeered when the convert died. There is a very similar story in Adomnán's account,[13] written only a century after it happened, of an incident in the sixth-century Pictish mission of Columba. Again Mrs Ling's experiences in the after-world, with the threatenings of demons, are closely paralleled in the experience of a seventh-century man who later became a monk in the Northumbrian monastery of Melrose. Bede, who recounts the story in considerable detail,[14] also tells of similar experiences in the life of Fursa, an Irish missionary to East Anglia.[15]

Healing: part of a charismatic package

We have noted the option (p. 131) of accepting the validity of miraculous healings but denying that they are examples (in post-apostolic days) of the charismata; that is the viewpoint of Sidlow Baxter in *Divine Healing of the Body*.[16] Certainly the Scottish reformers who were so signally blessed with miracles do not seem to have associated them with the promised gifts of the Holy Spirit. However, as we have seen in the case of John Welsh (pp. 82–5), many demonstrated the charismata in their own lives. It was not that they did not have them, they did not recognise them.

On the other hand the seventeenth-century Quakers did recognise facts. In *George Fox's Book of Miracles*,[17] which gives numerous case histories, the editor Henry Cadbury writes: 'The assurance of the sects that the powers of the apostolic age were being manifested in them led to a confidence in their contemporary ability to prophesy and work cures.' It is significant that when the rest of Fox's work was published this manuscript disappeared. It seems almost certain that the Society of Friends, like many Christians since, were too embarrased to admit to happenings which are intellectually unacceptable. Fortunately a list of contents was extant giving the first and last phrases of the case histories, and by painstaking detective work in the index of Fox's writings Cadbury reconstructed the volume.

The same applies to the other charismata, and as I maintain that they come as a package-deal we should spend a little time looking at them. While many delight to recall the nineteenth-century evangelistic missions of Dwight L. Moody, few refer to the fact that when he visited Sunderland there was an extraordinary scene in the YMCA of young men speaking in tongues.[18] We cannot see the point in them. It is agreed that at Pentecost the message in tongues was understandable to the listeners. Presumably, as they had come to Jerusalem, almost all of them would have understood Hebrew or Aramaic, but hearing it in their own language the good news became personally appropriate. The same may still be true. In January 1986 the following incident was told in Sunderland by two leaders of the Renewal in the Methodist church. I was not there but they have since confirmed it to me. Despondent with their work in the Christian ministry, John and Eileen Trevenna considered abandoning it; however they decided to go along to a service in a pentecostal church. They did not enjoy it and would have left had they not been hemmed in.

After some singing an old man at the front of the church

started to speak in a tongue and I felt myself going cold all over – I felt John going rigid at my side and it was if we were both rooted to the ground. [It should be mentioned that they had spent four years of their ministry in Ceylon – now Sri Lanka – and had learnt the language.] As we stood there in that church we heard the flowing tones in Sinhalese echoing round the building and the Lord speaking just to us through that old man. All of a sudden Acts 2:6 became real 'and everyone heard them speaking in his own language'. This wasn't something that only happened on the day of Pentecost, it's happening here and now.

From that moment there was no further talk of abandoning the ministry.

As far as we are concerned, let us be honest, it makes us hot under the collar. We do not like it. We get embarrassed. It upsets our equilibrium.

The Work of the Holy Spirit Today

But the Spirit is a wind (one Greek word in the New Testament has to do for both) – and not the gentle zephyr of our hymns. Acts 2:2 is variously translated as 'a rushing mighty wind' (AV), 'a violent wind' (NIV), 'a strong driving wind' (NEB). We are not talking about a soft breeze, not even a 'force 8 gale', but a 'force 10 storm'. Jesus reminded Nicodemus that the Spirit 'blows wherever it pleases' (John 3:8 NIV). God the Holy Spirit inconsiderately does not seem to be bothered by our desire for theological tidiness or respectability, or even denominational allegiance.

For too long God the Holy Spirit has been all but forgotten. I have got weary searching the indexes of volumes on my shelves. Take one example: *Historical Theology*[19] by William Cunningham, Principal of New College, Edinburgh, 1847–61; 1250 pages of text on 'the principal doctrinal discussions . . . since the apostolic age'. Its index runs to around 1100 entries;

there is a single item under 'Spirit', but nothing at all under Gifts, Charismata, Miracles, Healing; the word 'Church' lists 92 topics but includes none of the words we look for, even once. And Cunningham is not unique. Where the Holy Spirit's present work is discussed, the silence on his gifts is total. My generation of students was fortunate to be brought up on *In Understanding Be Men; a handbook of Christian doctrine for non-theological students*,[20] a splendid work which we tucked on our shelves between Jimmy's Anatomical Plates and Sammy Wright's Physiology. We are still lending out my wife's heavily underlined copy. In its twenty densely packed pages on the Person and work of the Holy Spirit there is no hint of a discussion of the charismata, unless it is in one of the twenty-seven set questions: 'Is the Holy Spirit functioning today as much as he was during the days of the Apostles? On what Scriptures or observations do you base your reply?' I am sure that as I worked through that magnificent volume in 1946 my answer to that question was 'No', but in 1986 I would answer, 'Yes: see evidence presented in my book.'

Perhaps we should not blame our earlier blindness, bearing in mind that our forebears in the faith were no more percipient. That first noble Confession of Faith, ratified by the Scots parliament on 17 August 1560,[21] says nothing whatever about the gifts of the Spirit, not even in the chapter on 'Faith in the Holy Ghost', unless it is in discussing the sacrament of the Lord's table: 'for the Holy Spirit, which can never be divided from the right institution of the Lord Jesus, will not frustrate the faithful of the fruit of that mystical action'. But wait, the final chapter is entitled, 'The Gifts freely given to the Kirk': here at last we must surely reach it. Alas, it deals solely with the topics (superb as they are) of remission of sins now, and glory hereafter. And, as I read it, the Anglican foundational document of the Thirty-Nine Articles is no improvement. How could they have been so blind?

Despite the deafening silence of generations of godly scholars it seems clear to me that the evidence of history and experience is that miraculous healings, and the other gifts of God the Holy Spirit, have continued (although at times more obviously than at others) from Pentecost until now without interruption. And this experience agrees with our Lord's promises.

The Exegesis of 1 Corinthians 13:8–12

A few opponents of the continuation of the charismata look for biblical support to Paul's first letter to the Corinthians where he interrupts his discussion on gifts with his praise of love, culminating in:

> Love never fails. But where there are prophecies, they will cease; where there are tongues, they will be stilled; where there is knowledge, it will pass away. For we know in part and we prophesy in part, but when perfection comes, the imperfect disappears. When I was a child, I talked like a child, I thought like a child, I reasoned like a child. When I became a man, I put childish ways behind me. Now we see but a poor reflection as in a mirror; then we shall see fact to face. Now I know in part; then I shall know fully, even as I am fully known. (NIV)

The gifts – prophecy, tongues, knowledge, and doubtless the rest – are therefore only temporary: to give way to something much better. Agreed; but when – down here or up there?

That situation they say has arrived; therefore there is no place now for the charismata. The idea that Paul thought we had reached perfection is flatly contradicted by his later statement when writing to the Philippians: 'Not that I have already obtained this or am already perfect; but I press on to make it my own, because Christ Jesus has made me his own' (3:12 RSV). Do we now know fully, as God knows us? Really? Is this the sharing of the divine splendour? Well, to be blunt, if that is the case then I am bitterly disappointed, I had hoped for more than this. Happily our disappointment is unnecessary for while there may be arguments on the continuation of the charismata worthy of careful consideration, that is not one of them.

There are others who use the same reasoning but apply 'that which is perfect' to the completed New Testament. (I am not sure that the completion of the canon was as early, or as clear-cut, as they appear to suggest.) The case is argued in detail in Victor Budgen's *Charismatics and the Word of God*.[22] As an exegesis of this part of 1 Corinthians 13, it is depressing. The hope of seeing our dear Lord face to face is diminished to a reference to an increasing knowledge of him through Bible study; worse – the wonderful expectation, 'Then shall I know even as I am known', is downgraded to mean merely, 'It is by the Word that *we know ourselves fully* as we are already known fully by God' (my italics). What a disappointment.

But not to worry. Having a free afternoon I spent it between the Dean and Chapter Library of Durham Cathedral, the library of St John's College, and two Christian bookshops. I managed to trawl twenty-three commentaries on the above passage, and that was the total bag, ranging from Cranmer (sixteenth century) to David Prior (1985). Not one of them so much as mentioned the idea that the completion of the scriptural canon fulfilled Paul's 'coming of completion'.

We are told that in the mid-eighteenth century Jonathan Edwards held this view. The fact however, far from supporting this strange exegesis, rather weakens it, for it follows that the idea has been known for more than two centuries, but not one of my unselected authorities had considered that it warranted a mention. I do not know Edwards' original work, but from Victor Budgen's chapter[23] (and he has a scholar's care for accuracy) it seems that Jonathan Edwards was writing, in the middle of the revival, to guard against extremes. His exegesis was very likely a finger-in-the-dyke first-aid measure. It has been resurrected today as a defence against current events which so many fear, but which many of us affirm to be miraculous.

Anyone who wants to explore Paul's meaning further could not do better than consult Dean Alford's Greek Testament.[24] Although first published in 1858, when a grateful patient gave me a set it was of the 1968 reprint, so important is it recognised to be for evangelical scholarship. Of this passage Alford writes: 'unquestionably the time alluded to is that of the coming of the Lord'.

Don Bridge (in *Signs and Wonders Today*)[25] examines this viewpoint in detail; sufficient to quote his, 'In fact the canon-of-Scripture argument as an end to the miraculous is a *non sequitur*. It brings the facts round in an absurd circle.' For what that completed New Testament brings is promise of the gifts, and instructions how to regulate them.

To me the real problem is the making of a false antithesis between holy Scripture and gifts. Both are the work of the same Holy Spirit: and presumably we grant that his right hand knows what his left hand is doing. Were it not for his inspiration and interpretation the Bible would be merely a fascinating book. Its unique character and importance is due solely to God the Holy Spirit. Because it is his principal means of communication, it becomes more valuable as the Holy Spirit takes control. It is a common experience that Christians who are renewed spend far more time reading Scripture than before, for we find it no longer merely a mine to be dug, an encyclopaedia to explore, a practice-and-procedure manual; it has become a teleprinter terminal on which the Holy Spirit prints individualised messages appropriate to our immediate circumstances.

While the Bible is the Holy Spirit's principal means of communication, it is not his only one, otherwise preaching, writing and evangelising would be a waste of time. Only if they too are energised by him can they be profitable. But what evidence is there that these exhaust his methods of reaching and teaching us?

The Gift of Prophecy

The Holy Spirit must also be able to speak specific words in the Christian's ear. 'Separate me Barnabas and Paul' (Acts 13:2). Do not preach in Asia or Bithynia (Acts 16:6–7). Down to earth detailed instructions of this kind cannot always be obtained by reading the words of Scripture. For this, one of

the ways he employs is prophecy. We must not allow the
service gifts of preaching and teaching, vital as they are to
the Church, to be foisted on us as this gift. In the divinity
student's manual, *A Theology of the New Testament*,[26] George
Eldon Ladd writes: 'Prophecy was not an office, but a gift
the Spirit could bestow on any member of the congregation.'
He was writing of the early Church, but the gift has not
changed. In a modern scholarly work, *New Heaven? New
Earth?*[27] Peter Hocken, a Roman Catholic, contributes a
chapter on 'The significance and potential of pentecostalism',
in which he quotes approvingly the following passage from
the presbyterian J. Rodman Williams:

> In prophecy God speaks. It is as simple, and profound,
> and startling as that! What happens in the fellowship is
> that the Word may suddenly be spoken by anyone present,
> and so, variously, a 'Thus says the Lord' breaks forth in
> the fellowship ... in prophecy God uses what He finds,
> and through frail human instruments the Spirit speaks the
> Word of the Lord.

This is not irrelevant to the subject of healing. We have seen
this gift in operation in Case Record 6.2 (p. 126) in the form
of 'a word of knowledge'.

It is customary in some circles to decry this gift, claiming
that as now practised it consists of a lot of generalised
quotations from Scripture. Often it does, but then how many
of the prophecies which fill the second half of the Old Testament were unique to the occasion? What was and is important
is the knowledge that *this* particular word of the Lord is being
given or emphasised specifically for *this* group and *this* time.
However on occasion it can be more direct. I recollect being
at a conference where prayer was offered for a couple who
were about to emigrate. Someone had a word from the Lord
which went something like this: 'When you arrive you will
meet a large warm-hearted Christian fellowship. I do not
want you to become members there. Later you will meet a
small uncongenial group of Christians: that is where you are
to throw in your weight for Me.' I have no idea what

happened, but I maintain that that is the gift of prophecy, still being given – as he gives the Bible – by the same donor.

Revivals of Religion

We have ample evidence in the Old Testament of specific times when God did remarkable things. Similarly in the Church age there have been times when he has been seen to be at work in unusual ways. We can read of this in the Reformation of the sixteenth century, the 'killing times' in seventeenth-century Scotland, the eighteenth-century evangelical revivals associated with the Wesleys in England, and their colleague Whitefield especially, north of the border. Mention of George Whitefield, however, reminds us of an alarming fact – that some Christians are unhappy about the company the Holy Spirit keeps. Just before his arrival in Scotland some of the most godly ministers had seceded from the established kirk. When a remarkable revival sprang up under William McCulloch, an ordinary parish minister, later joined by Whitefield, we would have imagined these seceding ministers to have been overjoyed. Not a bit of it. As Arthur Fawcett puts it in his doctoral study, *The Cambuslang Revival*,[28] 'The Seceders had decided, a priori that God could not bless this evangelist [Whitefield was an Anglican], minister of an uncovenanted church; this must therefore be a delusion, diabolically contrived.' They fasted against revival. And one seceding minister said: 'I will not believe any good fruits follow the ministry of such men as Whitefield, McCulloch, and others, tho' one that had been in the third heavens would say so.'

Believe it or not, the same is said about God's mighty works in the late twentieth century. As good a bench-mark as any other is to check what your sources say about his work through Kathryn Kuhlman.[29] Perhaps we should have been warned, for the New Testament records similar disapproval, by the religious purists of the day, of our Lord's company and behaviour.

In our generation there was a remarkable spiritual revival in the Outer Hebrides in 1949–53. The principal agent God used was Duncan Campbell, who, as a friend of my father's, was often in our home. To quote one of many instances, he writes, in *The Lewis Awakening*,[30] of a Church of Scotland elder on the tiny island of Bernera who, being in earnest prayer for that spiritually-dead island:

> was strangely moved, and enabled to pray the prayer of faith and lay hold upon the promise, 'I will be as the dew unto Israel.' This word from God came with such conviction and power, that he was assured that revival was going to sweep the island, and in that condition he rose from his knees. While [and I know Duncan Campbell meant the exact time] this man was praying in his barn, I myself, taking part in a convention at Bangor in Northern Ireland, was suddenly arrested by the conviction that I must leave at once and go to the Island of Bernera, where I found myself within three days! [Bearing in mind the transport facilities this was speedy indeed.] Almost immediately on arriving, I was in the midst of a most blessed movement. . . One evening, just as the congregation was leaving the church and moving towards the main road, the Spirit of God fell upon the people in Pentecostal power: no other words can describe it. . . There, under the open heavens and by the road side, the voice of prayer was mingled with the groans of the penitent. . . This movement was different from that in Lewis in this respect, that while in Lewis there were physical manifestations and prostrations, such were not manifested here; but the work was as deep and the results as enduring.

Campbell records numerous other dramatic episodes. What he has not recorded in print is that some of the most theologically orthodox ministers in the Long Isle forbade their members to attend his services, and some of them therefore came and listened through the windows. We find that at the time of the 'Cambuslang wark' some of the seceders likewise forbade their hearers either to read or to reason about the revival.[31]

I have mentioned earlier (pp. 35, 72) a remarkable work of the Holy Spirit in Plateau province, northern Nigeria, after we had left the area but while my sister and brother-in-law were there as senior missionaries. The major effects were conversion and spiritual renewal; however the gift of prophecy was widespread. This was exemplified in gifts of discernment. If any student made a public confession of sins, someone might butt in with: 'That is not all, you also have to confess. . .' naming specific sins hitherto unknown even to the interjector. In *The Wind Blowing*[32] our friends David and Bridget Williams recorded a fellow-missionary's comment:

It was just like the Acts of the Apostles, Chapter 2. One boy was so overcome that he rushed out of the hall shouting, 'Praise God I'm saved', and wanted to rush straight home, some twenty miles, to tell his parents what had happened to him. It appeared at first sight that he was drunk, but closer examination and talk showed the difference.

When they went home (for a holiday had to be called as so many students wanted to go home with their great news) some were said by their parents to be mad. One student reported:

As I reached my home town and started preaching I was thought to have been poisoned at school by some wicked friends. The Teachers' Training College captain travelled home to his own folk of the Angas tribe, visiting all the small centres, and taking as his text Joel 2:28: 'And it shall come to pass afterwards, that I will pour out my spirit upon all flesh; and your sons and your daughters shall prophesy, your old men shall dream dreams, your young men shall see visions.' (AV)

A member of John Wimber's[33] team said in November 1985, in my hearing, 'I asked the Lord if we were back to the days of the early apostles. But He said "No, you are into something bigger I have for you." ' Of course we have no means of knowing whether that prophetic word is for us – but today is, without any doubt, one of unusual activity on the part of the Holy Spirit.

It is time to give serious thought to the question with which we began this chapter. Are all these various blessings disconnected actions of God? A moment's thought will remind us that on planet Earth the executive member of the Godhead is the Holy Spirit. So he is doing them all: reformations, spiritual revivals, healings, gifts of prophecy, raising the dead. In such a time the old cliché is surely more than ever inappropriate: 'I seek the Giver, not the gifts'; thus effectively spurning both.

Of course we make a mess of things on the way, so everything is imperfect; pride, cowardice, self-seeking, acting on our own without his guidance; a thousand interferences have all occurred in every activity, and we can hurl bricks at each other like ticker-tape, but it does not invalidate the argument. More dangerously we can deny that some of these activities are God the Holy Spirit's work. That may be true here and there – people are healed in non-Christian religions, and by spiritualist mediums. But we must be very careful. It was the Pharisees' suggestion that a divine work was the work of devils that called down our Lord's most terrifying statement: 'Whosoever shall blaspheme against the Holy Spirit hath never forgiveness, but is guilty of an eternal sin' (Mark 3:29). It is not something I would like to chance.

We may not be very enthusiastic about what he is up to, but the Holy Spirit must be working to a plan. I take it we are agreed? None of us has been let into the secrets of the divine timetable, so we cannot be sure whether Joel 2:28–9 is finally being fulfilled or not. It is not important that we should know; all that is important is that we should make ourselves available as his instruments today.

1. B. B. Warfield, *Counterfeit Miracles*. 1918; reissued Edinburgh, Banner of Truth 1972.

2. H. J. Cadbury (ed.), *George Fox's Book of Miracles.* Cambridge University Press 1948; and New York, Octagon Press 1973.
3. Warfield, p. 245 n. 48.
4. E. Frost, *Christian Healing: a consideration of the place of spiritual healing in the Church today in the light of the doctrine and practice of the ante-Nicene Church.* London, Mowbray 1940.
5. M. Staniforth (tr.), *Early Christian Writing: the apostolic Fathers.* London, Penguin 1968.
6. G. A. Williamson (tr.), *Eusibius' History of the Church.* London, Penguin 1965.
7. V. Budgen, *The Charismatics and the Word of God* (Welwyn, Evangelical Press 1985), p. 120.
8. R. Markus, 'Lenten thoughts on Augustine'; on the 1600th anniversary of his conversion. *The Times*, 15 March 1986.
9. M. Kelsey, *Healing and Christianity: in ancient thought and modern times.* London, SCM 1973.
10. Augustine, *Concerning the City of God against the pagans*, tr. H. Bettenson; introd. J. O'Meara (London, Penguin 1984), pp. 1033–49.
11. 'Possidius' Life of S. Augustine', in F. H. Hoare (ed.), *The Western Fathers* (London, Sheed & Ward 1954), p. 231.
12. Augustine, op. cit. p. 1043.
13. A. O. and M. O. Anderson (eds), *Adomnán's Life of Columba* (Edinburgh, Nelson 1962), II.32.
14. *Bede's Ecclesiastical History of the English People*, ed. B. Colgrave and R. A. B. Mynors (Oxford, Clarendon Press 1969), V.12.
15. ibid. III.19.
16. J. S. Baxter, *Divine Healing of the Body.* Zondervan 1979.
17. Cadbury, op. cit. .
18. M. Harper, *As at the Beginning.* London, Hodder & Stoughton 1965.
19. W. Cunningham, *Historical Theology: a review of the principal doctrinal discussions in the Christian Church since the apostolic age.* 1862; reissued Edinburgh, Banner of Truth 1960.
20. T. C. Hammond, *In Understanding Be Men: a handbook of Christian doctrine for non-theological students.* London, Inter-Varsity Fellowship 1936.
21. This can be found in C. Lennox (ed.), *J. Knox: The History of the Reformation of Religion in Scotland* (London, Melrose 1905), App. 1.
22. Budgen, pp. 72–89.
23. ibid. pp. 165–78.
24. H. Alford, *The Greek Testament*, rev. E. F. Harrison. Chicago, Moody Press 1968.
25. D. Bridge, *Signs and Wonders Today* (Leicester, Inter-Varsity Press 1985), p. 136.
26. G. E. Ladd, *A Theology of the New Testament.* Grand Rapids, W. B. Eerdmans; and Guildford, Lutterworth 1974.

27. P. Hocken, in *New Heaven? New Earth? an encounter with pentecostalism.* A symposium. (London, Darton, Longman & Todd 1976), p. 24.
28. A. Fawcett, *The Cambuslang Revival: the Scottish evangelical revival of the 18th century.* Edinburgh, Banner of Truth 1971.
29. At Kathryn Kuhlman's great meetings in USA many people were healed.
30. D. Campbell, *The Lewis Awakening 1949–53* (Edinburgh, Faith Mission 1954), pp. 23–4.
31. Fawcett, p. 191.
32. D. and B. Williams, *The Wind Blowing* (Sidcup, Sudan United Mission 1973), pp. 24–7.
33. John Wimber, pastor of the rapidly growing Vineyard church in USA and lecturer in 'Signs and Wonders' at Fuller Theological Seminary, whose ministry is bearing remarkable fruit on both sides of the Atlantic.

8

Is the Christian entitled to claim Physical Healing?

If the gifts of God the Holy Spirit – including miraculous healings – are still being poured out in the late twentieth century, then surely healing is ours of right.

Health: a Christian's right?

That suggestion, or rather assertion, is frequently heard today. We must now check it out. A contemporary author writes: '*Lay aside your arguments from experience and look at what the Bible says about healing*; then you can learn to relate to your experience what God says'[1] (my italics). However, for reasons which I have spelt out in my introduction, I am unable to accept this approach, so I will use the same yardstick employed in Chapter 7: valid present-day experience. To quote the same author again: 'Your faith needs to be based on God's Word, not on facts. That does not mean that you deny the existence of the facts, but that you recognise *God has the power to change the facts*[2] (his italics). While agreeing with that last sentence I would maintain that the facts tell us what God is, indeed, doing in similar circumstances today. In essence the claim turns out to be that Christians have no need to be ill but are meant to live in good health to a ripe old age and then gently pass away. If we are to understand the arguments it is necessary to quote extensively.

For our first example we can take a fairly extreme view propounded in one of Kenneth Hagin's booklets.[3] He quotes from Deuteronomy 28, where the curses are listed, including

155

many named sicknesses, which God will allow to come upon
Israel if it backslides, and notes: 'The dreadful diseases specifically enumerated here – in fact every sickness and every
disease, according to the 61st verse – are part of the punishment for breaking God's law.' He makes the good point that
it is not that God sent them, 'but rather, when God's people
broke His commandments, they were out from under His
divine protection. And all He could do was permit the devil
to bring these afflictions upon them.' Sickness, then, is part
of the curse of the broken law, but 'Christ hath redeemed us
from the curse of the law' (Gal. 3:13 av). Hagin quotes with
approval someone who, caring for a woman moribund with
tuberculosis, instructed the patient to repeat to herself every
waking moment: 'According to Deuteronomy 28:22 consumption is a curse of the law. But according to Galatians 3:13
Christ has redeemed me from the curse of the law. *Therefore
I no longer have tuberculosis*' (my italics). She got better. Hagin
goes on to write, 'You can scripturally claim healing from
any sickness, because Deuteronomy 28:61 says *every sickness* is
a curse of the law. It will work for you too' (his emphasis).

For a much more mainstream view we can look at the work
of Colin Urquhart,[4] a clergyman whose parish was among
the first in England to experience the Holy Spirit's renewal
in these days, and who is one of the most respected leaders
in the charismatic movement. He reaches a rather similar
conclusion from a different starting point, retelling the story
of the leper who said to Jesus, 'Lord, if you will, you can
make me clean', with our Lord's reply, 'I will, be clean'
(Matt. 8:2–3). Urquhart continues:

> Here we see the Son speaking the words His Father gives
> Him to speak, and doing the works He saw His Father
> doing. Loving, Caring, Healing, Restoring, Meeting with
> the leper at the point of his need. Jesus didn't preach to
> him, He healed him! You need not doubt that God, your
> loving Father, desires to heal you. Either you have to say,
> 'God wants me to have this sickness', or you have to believe
> 'God does not want me to have this sickness'. If you think

He wants you to have it then you have no right to go to a doctor or try to lessen the pain, or even to pray about it. To do any of these things would be to go against what you say is God's will for you. This seems clearly ridiculous! He is certainly not a loving Father who wants to 'give good things' to His children if you think His best purpose for you is sickness and pain. So what is the alternative? He wants to heal!

Given these premises Urquhart goes on with sound advice:

In which case you have every right to pray; to ask, believing His promise; to seek the good offices of the medical profession. To believe God not only to alleviate the pain, but remove the disease, whether it is physical, mental or emotional; and to give you the healing you seek in the way He chooses.

We will come back to that phrase later, for I believe it to be vital in this whole field, but meanwhile we note that he suggests the involvement of the medical profession as well as faith.

Should We 'Take Authority' Over Disease?

However, with the certainty that God's will is present physical healing, there are those who can see no reason to involve medicine. Some approve of it, others do not, but with authority over disease why not get on and heal now?

The use of such authority is seen in the next case which I first read about in a leaflet. I would not have included it had not the patient, who is a medical practitioner, sent me a personal account. It turned out that among her friends is a family doctor, the godfather of one of my sons, from whom I was able to obtain some confirmation including the opinion that the patient is very level-headed 'and the very opposite of hysterical'.

CASE RECORD 8.1

The patient qualified in medicine at Sheffield in 1976. In January 1985, at the age of thirty-five, she became aware of some discomfort in her left breast, and two months later realised that there was a lump. She consulted her own general practitioner at the end of March, who confirmed the presence of a mass. He thought it was fibroadenosis (a benign condition) but referred her to a surgeon in case it was more serious.

'Personally, I was very shaken by the situation. I felt that the lump was progressively worsening. As time went on I found a tightness in my breast that made it uncomfortable to move my left arm. I developed a curious sensation like the involuntary contractions of a few fibres of the pectoral muscle. The area felt hot and this extended to the supraclavicular region. I am aware that this is subjective and some could be psychological. However it made me turn wholeheartedly to the Lord and trust Him to heal me.

'I attended a healing meeting in Runcorn, Cheshire, on 13 April.' The person ministering, a retired policeman, asked about her situation and then prayed: 'Thank you, Lord, for doctors and nurses and the work they do. If this is something cancerous, in the name of Jesus I command it to come out.' The patient continues: 'Immediately, I felt the lump come out and I felt the power of God come over me. Over the next few weeks I was more aware than usual of a spiritual battle and kept remembering that Jesus has the victory. The postal strike at that time delayed my hospital appointment and I therefore attended the hospital outpatients department on 1 May 1985. I saw a consultant surgeon at Chester Royal Infirmary who confirmed that the lump was gone, and discharged me from the clinic. The medical evidence may not seem very impressive. However, this experience has convinced me of the reality and power of the Lord Jesus to perform miraculous healings now.'

If that is how it can always be done, then are we not negligent if we allow any sick to remain in our congregations?

Is There Healing in the Atonement?

In this whole debate the crucial (in both senses of that word) theological issue centres on an episode which Matthew records early in Christ's ministry: 'When evening fell they brought to him many who were possessed by devils; and he drove the spirits out with a word and healed all who were sick, to fulfil the prophecy of Isaiah: "He took away our illnesses and lifted our diseases from us" ' (Matt. 8:16–17 NEB). (The reference is to Isaiah 53:4.) The disciples do not quote from the Hebrew version of the Old Testament, but usually from the Septuagint (LXX) a Greek translation of two hundred years earlier. But this verse is not quoted verbatim from the LXX for Matthew alters the vocabulary. Ray Hubbard, *Isaiah 53: is there healing in the Atonement?*[5] should be consulted by those who wish to probe the nuances of the Hebrew and Greek words employed.

It would be idle to deny that there are many difficulties in this passage. Did Christ on the cross bear not only our sins but also our sicknesses, and, if so, what are the implications for the Christian today? That is the crunch issue.

The facile interpretation of the verses, that they merely show that his life and ministry among the sick wearied and wore out our Lord, need not detain us. Most of us in medicine have felt like that after a hectic day in out-patients and theatre: especially when the phone rings again just when we have at last dropped off to sleep. And much the same could be said of numerous members of the other caring professions. There are many who would deserve such words. We can think of dozens of examples: Father Damien, nurse, priest and eventually fellow-sufferer with a thousand leprosy patients; Mother Teresa of Calcutta, a city whose sights revolted even the wartime serviceman, but are reputedly infinitely worse today.

Most pre-pentecostalist biblical commentators have not considered this passage worthy of discussion. However, to his credit, A. B. Bruce, Professor of Theology in Glasgow a century ago, in a famous work, *The Training of the Twelve*,[6] went deeper when he wrote:

> The devout Matthew, according to his custom, saw in these wondrous works Old Testament Scripture fulfilled; and the passage whose fulfilment he found therein was that touching oracle of Isaiah, 'Surely He hath borne our griefs and carried our sorrows'; which, departing from the Septuagint, he made apt for his purpose by rendering, 'Himself took our infirmities and bore our sicknesses.' The Greek translators interpreted the text as referring to men's spiritual maladies – their sins; but Matthew deemed it neither a misapplication nor a degradation of the words to find in them a prophecy of Messiah's deep sympathy with such as suffered from any disease, whether spiritual or mental, or merely physical. He knew not better how to express the intense compassion of his Lord towards all sufferers, than by representing Him in prophetic language as taking their sicknesses on Himself. Nor did he wrong the prophet's thought by this application of it. He but laid the foundation of an *a fortiori* inference to a still more intense sympathy on the Saviour's part with the spiritually diseased.

Involvement in our suffering: yes. Compassion: yes. But surely there has got to be more to Matthew's verses than that. From Hubbard's meticulous linguistic study it seems that the passage really insists that what Christ did for our sins he did for our sicknesses. But, as Tolkien's Treebeard would say, let's not be hasty.

Among the splendid new songs that the Lord is giving the Church in these days is one which contains the lines:

> Over sin He has conquered,
> Over death victorious,
> Over sickness He has triumphed.
> (*The Servant King*, 1985 suppl.)

While it is usually unwise to build theological doctrine on hymnology, I believe that here Graham Kendrick's parallelism leads us into the correct interpretation of this verse.

Our Lord has indeed achieved all these things, but into none of them do we fully enter until we see him face to face.

Now: but not yet

Sin conquered? Yes. Paul spelled it out to the Colossian believers:

> When you were dead in your sins and in the uncircumcision of your sinful nature, God made you alive with Christ. He forgave us all our sins, having cancelled the written code, with its regulations, that was against us and that stood opposed to us; he took it away, nailing it to the cross. *And having disarmed the powers and authorities, he made a public spectacle of them, triumphing over them by the cross.* (Col. 2:13–15 NIV). (my italics)

Marvellous! And no doubt that is how they see it throughout the galaxies.

Sin defeated? I have to admit that is not startlingly obvious in my ante-natal clinics, where in the last two years the proportion of patients having documented evidence of pre- or extra-marital conceptions has, on occasion, risen to 70 per cent. And it is no easier to believe in my gynaecological out-patients when the middle-aged wife of a homosexually-inclined man presents herself terrified of having contracted AIDS; and a tearful mum brings her pregnant fourteen-year old daughter beseeching abortion. It is equally difficult for any of us to believe when we read in our newspapers a daily catalogue of murder, rape, hijack, riot, baby-battering; or as horror-struck we watch on our TV screens the starvation of whole tribes of people.

Can we find some hint towards a resolution of our dilemma: Christus victor yet the devil rampant? My generation may find help in recalling June 1944. I was then in the South-East Asia theatre of war. Later the 14th Army commander, Field-Marshal Slim, was to write of that month, 'The Imphal-Kohima battle, the first decisive battle of the Burma

161

campaign, was not yet over, but it was won.'⁷ At the same time, far away in Europe, the Allies achieved their second front with the landings in Normandy: the long awaited D-Day. There was still a huge amount to do, the German armies were still in the field, the Rhine barrier would have to be crossed, Berlin was a long way off; but despite all this we knew that we had the victory. V-Day came, a year and much toil later. It may help if we reckon, imperfect as the analogy is, that in the cosmic war we Christians live between D-Day and V-Day.

In other words we live in a now-but-not-yet situation. This is well demonstrated in a passage in Paul's letter to the Hebrews: 'because by one sacrifice he has made perfect for ever those who are being made holy' (10:4 NIV). This chronological tension is also present in the preceding verse which reminds us that Christ is seated at the right hand of God waiting for his enemies to be made his footstool.

We get the same idea in Paul's letter to the Ephesians where he counsels them about present problems in their family life, their church life, and in the danger of contamination with pagan thought-patterns. But Paul sets all this against a statement which is breathtaking in the audacity of its tenses:

> God, rich in mercy, for the great love he bore us, brought us to life with Christ even when we were dead in our sins; it is by his grace you are saved. And in union with Christ Jesus he raised us up and enthroned us with him in the heavenly realms, so that he might display in the ages to come how immense are the resources of his grace, and how great his kindness to us in Christ Jesus. (2:4–7 NEB)

When the Ephesian Christians were tempted, as they were, with fornication and indecency, when the strain of their slave-master relationship was wearing them down, they were to remind themselves of their present cosmic status. I do not know that Paul got round to advising them to put on their mantelshelves a reminder, 'Keep looking down', but that is the thrust of his early chapters. It is where Christians are:

seated with Christ, the victory having been achieved – but in the middle of a battle.

Let us be honest; have I been toying with words which really add up to 'sin is not defeated'? Is all this in fact whistling in the dark? Far from it. For although sin in our neighbours, sin in our environment, still remain and the Christian is not preserved from the results of sin in society, domestic burglary or global war; we are confident because we know that God 'rescued us from the domain of darkness and brought us away into the kingdom of his dear Son, in whom our release is secured and our sins forgiven' (Col. 1:13–14 NEB). The Christian has a new citizenship and as a member of God's family does not have to yield to sin, does not have to be defeated by temptation, is no longer subject to Satan and can in fact, in the name of the Lord Jesus, command him to depart for the time being.

James Dunn, in his study, *Jesus and the Spirit*,[8] puts it this way:

> The proclamation [by Jesus] of the end-time's imminence was nothing new; it was the proclamation of its presence which was so astonishing. What on earth could make Jesus think the kingdom was already present, when the claim was contradicted on every side? The answer lies in the presence of one element, a key-characteristic of the end-time – the plenitude of the Spirit's power. . . *The already-not-yet tension in Jesus' proclamation stems immediately from his consciousness of Spirit.* (his italics)

So we have not wandered far from our subject of sickness. At the beginning sickness resulted from sin, that is how it entered the world. And so also did death. 'It was through one man that sin entered the world, and through sin death, and thus death pervaded the whole human race, inasmuch as all men have sinned' (Rom. 5:12 NEB). But having made this point Paul later wrote to Timothy of 'our Saviour, Christ Jesus, who has destroyed death' (2 Tim. 1:10). Despite that completed deed it is not until we turn to the penultimate

163

chapter of the Bible that we reach 'there shall be an end to death' (Rev. 21:4).

Satan and his agents, sin, sickness, death, have been conquered by Christ, but until the end of this age they remain still present and active. It would be great if that was not the case. We long to be in heaven where there will be none of these things. The problem is that, while realising that we will have to wait till then for the other liberations of glory, we really want our resurrection bodies *now* and are dissatisfied that we have not got them. Paul felt the same:

> We groan indeed, we who are enclosed within this earthly frame; we are oppressed because we do not want to have the old body stripped off. Rather our desire is to have the new body put on over it, so that our mortal part may be absorbed into life immortal. God himself has shaped us for this very end; and as a pledge of it he has given us the Spirit. (2 Cor. 5:4–5 NEB)

But a pledge is a promise of something for which we still have to wait. This is true even when the Holy Spirit does heal us, for (in Walter Stockdale's percipient phrase) when he does, he heals us into dying bodies.

Mind you, even here and now, sometimes we do better than we expect.

CASE RECORD 8.2

A fellow conference member told me this story in October 1984 as we jolted by bus to Mysore. It was a long trip and there was time to talk at a deep level. She is a Roman Catholic, middle-aged, and had been troubled with back pains for some years. During Francis McNutt's visit to Bombay in the 1970s she attended one of his meetings, after much cajoling by one of her relatives. A woman went up on to the platform to ask for prayer for her back-ache. My friend was embarrased to follow that example, but reasoned that the Lord could hear her prayer where she sat. So she asked him. Her back ache was healed and has remained so, as our day's trip gave ample evidence to prove. However she had discovered simultaneously that the urinary stress-incontinence which had troubled her for a long time, but for which she had not prayed for healing, had also completely disappeared and had not recurred. When asked to heal one problem God cured two!

Does Faith Guarantee Healing?

That God can heal miraculously there is no doubt: if you do not accept this, turn to Case Record 10.4 (p. 202) before you throw the book away.

That God does heal in the late twentieth century should be accepted on the evidence of all these Case Records.

If you do not accept those two statements, you may ask yourself what evidence you would be prepared to accept. If the answer proves to be 'None', then you had better face the fact that you have abandoned logical enquiry.

However we are committed to logical enquiry so the next question must be, 'Does God in fact heal everyone who asks, or for whom healing is asked from him?' And the answer has to be no. It is an unpopular answer with those who have built up a theological argument, such as that of the author quoted at the beginning of this chapter, or one of the numerous schema built on other texts but all reaching the same conclusion: God can heal you, he wants to heal you, believe it, claim it, and it will happen.

It sound great, but sometimes it does not work. To be honest: frequently it does not work. Figures? In the field of healing probably no name is more respected than that of Francis McNutt. From his experience he believes in prolonged 'soaking' prayer. In a letter to me in June 1985 he writes:

As for the people we pray for; it does seem to me that *most* who have organic disease experience at least some degree of improvement. If we pray for, say, ten people in an hour's period (provided they have the kind of sickness we can check out on the spot), one or two will be completely healed, five or six improved, and for the others not much will happen. *Mostly* what we see is improvement – which usually means that if we had more *time*, they probably can be totally healed.

There are, beyond reasonable disbelief, many astounding cases. Only recently a GP friend attended a healing conference where he saw a phlegmatic Yorkshire lass bounding up and down with joy. She had had a back condition requiring spinal fusion, apparently at more than one level, with the insertion of orthopaedic pins or plates, as a result of which she could only stand absolutely erect, bending was impossible. And there he saw her, crying with joy, up and down touching her toes. I cannot use this as one of my Case Records as I have no other details, but my friend – who has long experience of this ministry – was completely convinced. However the point to be made is that during four days of conference that was the only dramatic cure he saw personally. That is not to imply that others did not occur: indeed another friend (also a family doctor) at the same conference told me of other cases including one so astounding that, in the absence of name, address or confirmable medical details, I dare not print it. But there must have been large numbers among the thousands attending who were not healed. Why?

People are not healed – so the commonest explanation runs – because they do not have enough faith. There are three important reasons why this explanation is unacceptable.

1. If adequate faith brings down my healing then I have been the vital agent in the healing, not God. I deserve congratulation. 'You didn't think I had it in me did you? I'm more spiritual than you imagined. All those others weren't healed but I was, so there!' Of course we would not dream of saying that, we will even try not to think that, but. . . In Pauline vocabulary – healing has been of work: the very hard work I had in screwing up enough faith, and hanging on to it like grim death. And as my faith proved sufficient, then,

along with great gratitude to God, surely just a little self-congratulation is not out of place?

2. If faith mandates healing, then God is no longer Sovereign. God has become a dispensing-machine. Insert the appropriate amount of faith, pull the lever, and there is the healing. He has no choice, whatever he knows might be for the best as he longs for me in love, bears in mind my situation, and sees my future. All that is irrelevant. His hands are tied. (My parents told me a story of missionary acquaintances – I have no means of confirmation so this is merely quoted as an anecdote – the couple in question had a child who developed cerebral meningitis and became desperately ill. The parents demanded of God that he saved their child's life. He did, but they were left to care long-term for what we would class, in medical parlance, a vegetable.)

3. Much the most important: this explanation is unacceptable because it is not true. There are multitudes of cases of people with sublime faith who have not been healed: we will look at a couple shortly. Meanwhile I recall the minister of my own church who developed a cerebral tumour. His faith and that of the fellowship were very great. He did surprisingly well and on being allowed home from the regional neurological unit his instruction to the congregation was, 'Stop praying, and start praising!' It was seventy-two hours later that he had his fatal haemorrhage into the neoplasm. Such had been the faith that I felt it wise to get sight of the post-mortem report lest the Lord had indeed, in response to faith, removed the new growth, but then for his own purposes taken him home through some other mechanism. But that had not been the case.

It proves that God's plan is not always our return to full health. A lady sent me the following account, via the BBC.

At a time when my correspondent had, as I understand, little Christian commitment, she was very upset by the news that the six-year-old child of an acquaintance was ill in hospital with an inoperable tumour of the brain, unable to walk, speak or swallow. She shared this distress with her daughter who lived elsewhere. The latter replied, 'Don't worry any more, Mum. Our Christian group will pray for her twice a week and she will be cured.' She goes on: 'She was so certain. And so it was. From then on the whole group (about 200 people) began to pray for the child and it was then she began to get better. She is now back at school and fights with her brother again . . . I feel knocked sideways. It is so wonderful. Can it really be true that Jesus lives?'

I was able to confirm the unexpected and dramatic recovery with the teaching hospital concerned. More than a year later I wrote to the consultant for the latest news, and learned that the child had had a relapse a few months earlier, and had died.

What are we to make of that history? Remission? Could be, but as a total explanation I do not think, if we are honest, that explanation will satisfy us. I cannot pretend to be able to explain what God was doing in this case. The idea that he gave up on the cure because the group perhaps gave up their prayers gets us back into the 'healing by works' bondage we have already dismissed above. I can only suggest that he responded to the faith of the Christian lass, and then, in due course, carried out the plan he had seen was best from the beginning. We have been comforted, when the Lord got impatient to welcome our own little son Alistair, that in God's city the streets are full of boys and girls playing (Zech. 8:5). We come once again to the place where we have always got to stand – God loves us, he watches over us, individually, constantly, 168 hours a week.

For all these reasons we must never, in an circumstances whatever, allow the 'insufficient-faith' explanation to be offered. It is a cop-out, however elegant the theological edifice from which it is pronounced. But there is another extremely important reason why it must be rejected. It may let the would-be healer, or the spiritual adviser, or 'friends', off the hook; but it is very likely to impale the patient on a bigger one.

For inevitably – and how could it be otherwise – day after day after day, their mind will go round in circles: 'I really did believe the Lord would heal me, but he hasn't. I read in that book, "When you look at things from God's perspective, you realise sickness is no problem for Him. It is not difficult for God to heal cancer, to straighten twisted limbs, or to heal the broken-hearted. But He does want faith to work with."[9] So it's obvious. I couldn't have had enough faith. It's clear that I was kidding myself before when I used to think his loving arms were round about. me. I'm obviously spiritually a third-class citizen and I mustn't ever delude myself again that I am close to the Lord, or that he really cares that much about me. And then I've been let down so badly by my friends. They all said they would pray and trust. Fine words! Quite clearly they can't have bothered if between them all they could not accumulate enough faith-tokens to get me healed. So now I know how much to value their so-called friendship and prayer-support.'

Such resulting loneliness and despair can overshadow a Christian's last days with gloom. I have known it happen. I also know someone in my own profession who, because faith did not produce the cure which a patient's theology demanded, now proclaims himself an agnostic and has completely abandoned the Christian gospel he once preached in Britain and in the mission field.

God's Different Plans

But it is time to support by two examples my argument that God does not necessarily grant physical healing in response to believing prayer. As both have been published there is no need to employ professional anonymity.

Joni Eareckson. This horse-riding, lacrosse-playing, sports-car driving American girl broke her neck and became paraplegic (totally paralysed below that spot) at the age of seventeen. Her own account, *Joni,*[10] with its honest account of her

169

bitterness, anger, and eventual trust in the loving God who had 'allowed' this to happen, is perhaps the most moving autobiography of the last decade. It is made all the more challenging by the beautiful sketches, drawn using a brush held between her teeth, and each signed 'Joni PTL' (PTL – Praise the Lord).

In the second volume, *A Step Further*,[11] she reports that she received, and still gets, large numbers of letters telling her that she could be healed. Among those she quotes is this:

> John 10:10 says we are to have an abundant life. Being paralysed, can you honestly say you are having an abundant life? Jesus came to set people free. You're bound to your wheelchair. Your body is the temple of the Holy Spirit. Do you think He wants His temple to be broken and helpless?

Joni writes: 'These points which others have shared seemed to make sense. Guess that answers my question about where I should go from here, I thought to myself. Having considered the issue I became convinced healing was for me.'

So in 1972 a group of close friends, family and church leaders met in a church. They read together the scriptural promises for healing, they anointed her with oil.

> Then followed a time of direct, fervent believing prayer for my healing. We asked God to glorify Himself by allowing me to walk again, and we trusted Him to do so . . . I left the church parking lot in exactly the same frame of mind that I had entered it – fully expecting God to heal me. 'Thank You, Lord,' I prayed silently as the car pulled out, praising God for what I was convinced He had already begun to do.

Weeks and months passed: no healing. Why? It may be easy for the thousands of people, on both sides of the Atlantic, especially the young, who have been blessed by her books and challenged by her wheelchair appearances, to see some explanation why God did not grant those prayers. But Joni's own exploration of all this should be studied.

David Watson saw the Lord bless his ministry, building up his congregation in York a hundredfold, from 7 to 700. Often taking with him a team from the fellowship of St Michael-le-Belfrey, he conducted missions in all parts of the world, especially among students. The notes scribbled on the end-papers of my Bible are of readings on 'Christ the Healer', which he gave at the Christian Medical Fellowship conference in Wharfedale, ten years ago. In 1983, five days before he was due to take his team to the west coast of America, he was diagnosed as having bowel cancer. In the next twelve months he wrote *Fear no Evil: a personal struggle with cancer*.[12] At surgery liver secondary involvement was found, so the condition was beyond medical cure. Three friends immediately flew from America to pray with him, including John Wimber (see p. 154 n. 33). They went straight from Heathrow to David's hospital side ward. He writes:

> As we talked, they sensed the power of God coming upon them, so they began to pray. They praised God for his presence with us, for his authority over life and death, and they prayed against the spirit of unbelief, fear and death that was pervading the room. . . I felt a tremendous surge of heat as well as vibrations in my body, and I knew that God was at work. This went on for half an hour or more, and we all had no doubt that God was with us.

He died thirteen months after the diagnosis was made, and five weeks after completing his manuscript. The book is a study of the problems surrounding suffering and healing and, like Joni's, is mandatory reading for anyone who wants to understand what it is like to be at the sharp end. Read with awe.

Another explanation occasionally offered for failure of cure is that the person must be demon-possessed. I do not propose to discuss the question of demonology but I do not deny that this explanation might be true in a very few cases. But when the most Christ-like person I have ever met was not healed and possible demon-possession was suggested, I (like many others who knew him far better than I did) had great difficulty in not blowing a fuse. When theological dogma requires to be shored up by such desperate measures then the time to re-examine its validity is overdue.

Should We Disregard Remaining Symptoms?

Most worrying of all is the dictum: 'You are healed although the symptoms have not disappeared; disregard them.' A personal attempt to practise this on one occasion ended disastrously. We note that, because he was sick, Trophimus was left at Miletus, while Paul went on (2 Tim. 4:20). Why did he not tell himself, 'I'm healed', pack his kit and travel with Paul? This dictum is worrying because it seems downright dishonest, and it is not immediately obvious how we can honour God by using lies. The non-Christian, seeing the person who is clearly still as ill as before proclaiming, 'I am healed', is quite right to roar with laughter, although hopefully he does not do so until he is outside the room and recounting the tale to his friends. If he scorns such a faith and the God who works like that, I for one will not blame him. Diseases are diagnosed principally on symptoms: if they persist the disease persists. It is as easy as that. Let us stop calling black white, ostensibly to protect the good name of the Lord, but in reality to get ourselves out of an embarrassing situation, and – even worse – from having to rethink our dicta.

This view is not only worrying because it is dishonest but, worse, because it can be highly dangerous. Some years ago one of the Sunday newspapers ran a piece about a district in the American mid-west where a considerable number of children (amounting to a score, if my memory serves) died because their parents were told to discontinue medication after healing services. Medicines are part of God's provision, and to be taken with thankfulness, in parallel with prayer. (Admittedly this fouls up any attempt to 'prove' miraculous healing when the criteria demand that there should be no concomitant medication, but such demands are based on

172

inadequate theological understanding of God's work: creation ordinances, in the jargon.)

There is another practical danger, instanced by Professor Rendle Short,[13] one of the patriarchs of organised Christian witness in the medical world. In a talk to his students on faith-healers he said:

> Patients who derive no benefit, or who later relapse, may suffer a serious eclipse of faith concerning things spiritual as well as temporal. In one case a young woman suffering from pulmonary tuberculosis, who had been under the care of a medical relative of mine and for whom a bed at a sanatorium had been reserved, went to a faith-healing mission. She thought she had been cured and refused the bed. Months later, when she was much worse, she requested admission. *But how many of her relatives had she infected in the interval?* (my italics)

The last explanation we need to consider is that the healing is on the way, and will occur, although either gradually or after the passage of time. I am sure this is often the case. However 'hope deferred maketh the heart sad' and we must be careful not to delude ourselves, or the sufferer.

There is one more explanation: the Lord has other plans. We will be looking at that finally, in Chapter 10.

1. C. Urquhart, *Receive your Healing* (London, Hodder & Stoughton 1986), p. 22.
2. ibid. p. 44.
3. K. E. Hagin, *Redeemed: from poverty . . . sickness . . . death*, 7th edn. Tulsa, Kenneth Hagin Evangelistic Assoc. 1975.
4. C. Urquhart, *Anything you Ask*. London, Hodder & Stoughton 1978.
5. R. Hubbard, *Isaiah 53: is there healing in the atonement?* Bromley, Foundation Publications 1972.
6. A. B. Bruce, *The Training of the Twelve*, 6th edn (Edinburgh, Clark 1924), p. 48.
7. Sir W. Slim, *Defeat into Victory* (London, Cassell 1956), p. 346.
8. J. D. G. Dunn, *Jesus and the Spirit* (London, SCM 1975), p. 89.
9. Urquhart, *Receive your Healing*, p. 88.

10. J. Eareckson, *Joni.* Glasgow, Pickering & Inglis; and Zondervan 1976.
11. id. and S. Eves, *A Step Further* (Glasgow, Pickering & Inglis 1979; and Zondervan 1978), pp. 122–4.
12. D. Watson, *Fear no Evil: a personal struggle with cancer.* London, Hodder & Stoughton 1984.
13. W. M. Capper and D. Johnson (eds),.*The Faith of a Surgeon: belief and experience in the life of Arthur Rendle Short* (Exeter, Paternoster 1976), p. 89.

9

God's Strange Work

'God's outlandish work.' This phrase used by Isaiah (28:21 NEB) in a completely different context, nevertheless seems most appropriate with which to introduce a chapter I would gladly have omitted: a course I was strongly advised to follow by those whose opinion I respect. However a study such as this demands intellectual integrity. If the following accounts are uncongenial is it because my world-view, even my Christian world view, is shattered, and that I am embarrased when God oversteps the mark?

In his seminal book, *Healing*,[1] Francis McNutt includes an epilogue entitled, 'The story of the three Indians'. He had planned this as the first chapter but his publishers maintained that it was a bit too much to expect the average person to believe, and that therefore they might lose most readers before they got past the first chapter. No wonder! It is the story of three Sioux Indians who came to a South Dakota monastery while McNutt was visiting, to report that they had recently experienced healing. I will relate two incidents.

One Indian reported visiting Minneapolis the previous Sunday. Her boy said, 'Mom, I got a toothache. They have a healing service over there. Why don't we go?' She continued: 'So we went over there. He went up and this man prayed for him. And right there Jesus filled seven of his teeth that had cavities. He filled them with silver. This is really so. That is how powerful Jesus is. . .'

Then a second Indian, Nancy, a shy girl of about twenty, gave a similar testimony but in her case the healing did not start from her faith:

175

I didn't believe that Jesus can heal anybody... I was sitting there, and the man that was standing up there come up to me and told me to come up to the front. He said 'You don't believe: you never did really accept Jesus. I want to pray for you.' I didn't say nothing, I just stood there. He said, 'Do you have any fillings?' I said, 'No.' He said, 'Do you have any cavities?' I said, 'Yes, but I am going to go to a dentist.' He said, 'Well, I am going to pray for you. I want you to put your mind on Jesus. Forget everything else.'

Francis McNutt reports Nancy's testimony of a peculiar sensation, after which she found, and later confirmed in a mirror, that she now had silver and gold fillings.

This whole episode is, of course, too laughably ridiculous to warrant a moment's belief, or would be if it were not reported by the doyen not only of writers, but of workers in this field. Even so there are surely limits to our credulity.

The Service at Labranza

First witness. In 1976, two years after that account was published, the British magazine *Crusade* carried an article by John Pridmore,[2] chaplain to an English school, who had just been on a visit to South America. He made it clear at the time that he was not happy with the inescapable implications of the events he was himself recording. In 1985 he wrote to me:

I'd like to think that the article remained a fair account of what happened – except 'what happened', if indeed it was a miracle, is going to elude description, such are the linguistic and philosophical problems posed by any attempt to describe anything outside one's normal experience. I've never seen anything like it since. As the years pass I am more of the opinion that such events raise such huge moral and theological difficulties that one rather hopes it was conjuring rather than divine intervention.

First, then, for John Pridmore's report, and then confirmatory accounts, which should allay any reasonable doubts.

CASE RECORD 9.1

The tiny church was crowded. It can hold about fifty in comfort but tonight, in some discomfort, three times that number are here. It is winter and to keep the heat in, all the windows are closed. As a visitor you are bound to be aware of the smell (or smells, for there are several). But a moment's reflection makes you ashamed you noticed. Fastidiousness in such matters is after all a first-world luxury for those who can afford hot baths.

The church is a simple building. A plain wooden structure, bare walls and floor, rough benches and rough table, made with little art but much love, and achieving in its poverty and austerity an extraordinary dignity. Those who worship here are very poor but they have built a house of prayer that draws you to your knees. . .

The evangelist's sermon ends, as it began, in prayer. Now those who wish to commit their lives to Christ are invited to repeat his prayer after him. Many accept this invitation. One voice disturbs and distresses me. A child is praying and his high-pitched, hysterical voice mounts above the others. The fathomless grief of this little boy's prayer appals me. What has this long, hot, emotional night done to this child? Someone, please stop him. Take him out, comfort him. I am angry that the vulnerability of a child should be so exploited. But the weeping child continues his bitter prayer and no one seeks to silence him.

Now those who look for healing are asked to pray for it. The evangelist and the pastor lay hands on some, but there are so many they cannot touch them all. 'Put your hand where you need healing,' says the evangelist. And all around the little church these simple folk place their own hands where they most suffer.

Now you see what is the most common and the most cruel of the physical afflictions of these needy people. For most in this meeting are touching their teeth. All the missionaries hereabout confirm the truth of this. Deficiencies in diet are such that tooth decay is so prevalent as to be almost universal. (Some might say there are worse maladies than bad teeth but those who say so are usually not suffering from toothache at the time.)

So the prayer for healing is offered. And now those who already know that this prayer is answered are invited to tell us, to show us, what has happened. Because the evangelist sees in me a sceptical European I am summoned to the platform to see for myself the works of God. Doubting Thomas is not allowed to lurk in a corner. With the assistance of the evangelist's torch (who, expecting great things from God, has come prepared) I look into their mouths one after another.

And I know what I see is a miracle. For these folk never go to the dentist. The poor of Chile are poor beyond our imagination. Dental treatment is entirely beyond their means and the only treatment, could they afford it, is extraction. But these teeth have been filled. And the filling has the form of a silver cross set in each tooth.

One little boy – and although he is in rags, I do not think I have seen a child so happy – shows me his teeth. Several are filled with what looks like silver. But God keeps his best gifts for children and this little one can show me a tooth into which is set, delicately but quite distinctly, a golden cross. It is this boy, now so radiant, who minutes previously had so upset me by his anguished prayer. . .

Second witness. Dr Bill Maxwell (who is now in practice in London) and his wife were missionaries at that place at the time, and I have been able to talk to them. He stayed at home baby-sitting that night, but Mrs Maxwell, a trained nurse, was present and confirmed to me having examined at least one man who had a tooth filled then.

Third witness. Miss Kath Clark, another member of the South American Missionary Society (an Anglican organisation) was also there. She was in the habit of posting back to Britain tape-recordings of their work, and has tracked down and sent me the tape for that week. It is a moving experience to eavesdrop on such an occasion.

We are in an evangelistic service in a little church called Labranza and this is the opening hymn of this service and I will play different parts of the service to you as we go along. It is a very small village outside Temuco and the church has been put up now for just six days. They have been celebrating these days with an evangelistic campaign. 'God is in this place/ God is in this place/ The Holy Spirit is revealing to me that God is in this place.' These are the words of the chorus they are singing and there is a tremendous sense of expectancy and sense of faith as everyone, as it were, is concentrating on the fact of the presence of God with them and so the expectation that God is going to work, going to do things in lives tonight is very high. The evangelist who will be preaching later on is a Chilean called Alejandro Sigel.

The congregation is reading Psalm 103 together. Quite a lot of the people cannot read. Clarissa Figaroa is the girl who has been the mainstay, in a sense, of a little church along the coast . . . one of the things the Lord has done is to give Clarissa the melody and the words of this beautiful song which she is singing now. . . The Lord is holy. Alleluia/ The Lord is holy. Alleluia./ And he is doing marvels in my life here and now/ The Lord is holy. Alleluia/ I want to go and dwell with him in his kingdom.

The next bit will be just a few words of the preaching of Brother Alejandro. . . You see the active vital participation at every point of the congregation with whatever is happening.

[Miss Clark continues, obviously next day:] Brother Sigel continued to preach and made an appeal. A number of people went forward. He clearly counselled them, and after there was another appeal for those who were seeking healing because Sigel believes very firmly that when the kingdom of God comes there should be accompanying signs. The incredible thing is that after prayer for healing, many people, it seems so strange this, many people wanted healing of different ills that they had, but a large number of people had tremendous toothache because they just cannot ever get to a dentist, and the dental state of so many of the poorer people is just desperate. That night I saw various new fillings, teeth that had not been filled were filled. (And the following night, I understand that a new tooth was actually created. Somebody had a gap then had a tooth. It seems so incredible and yet, there it is, it happens.)

In fact the night of that meeting I have recorded I was asked to go forward and give a testimony because I had got lots and lots of stoppings and suddenly they had all gone bright and shiny. I just could not believe it could happen to me. I had prayed so much for other people and yet an earlier night in the campaign when we had been praying for healing, I had felt a tremendous warmth all round my jaws and a burning, burning sensation. I did not think any more about it. I did not bother to look in a mirror or anything. But two or three days later I just realised that there was something that was shining in my mouth. And there, lo and behold, the same old stoppings, or where the old stoppings were, still stopped, but in a new bright shining material. It's incredible so all I can do is to give thanks and praise to God, and perhaps it is to help some of you realise that really it is happening.

Further Case Histories

Dr Maxwell, in a letter to me, comments:

I have taken a photo of one tooth filled, but it is a very amateur shot which would hardly be worth much in evidence, except I was convinced enough to have a try! The Church accepted that Jesus healed so there was no special notice taken of teeth filling. It just fitted in with all the other miracles.

What are we to make of these bizarre stories? Of their veracity I have no doubt. John Pridmore points to one huge problem: 'A god who gives hungry people teeth rather than food is, to say the least, pretty unattractive.' That question we will address later (p. 184) but the quotation shows that we are not dealing with exuberant gullible witnesses.

CASE RECORD 9.2

Miss Kath Clark writes to me of an eleven-year-old girl from the village of Chol Chol in southern Chile who was known to have spent time knocking at the doors of neighbours in the village asking for aspirin because of the severe pain she was experiencing because of bad teeth. 'An Indian Mapuche Lay Reader and I prayed for her in the context of an evangelistic service when at one point we broke into groups to pray for each other. The Mapuche evangelist was praying very much that he would receive a new middle front tooth because he did a lot of preaching and found it quite difficult with this tooth missing. However, we both prayed for the child who was in agony with her toothache. We sensed a tremendous warmth and presence of the Lord and she said her mouth was burning, then we looked in and saw that where there had been dark decay and in some places no teeth at all, the decayed areas had been filled with beautiful stoppings with little silver crosses on, and in areas where there were no teeth at all she was sensing pain as well. (We subsequently found that new teeth had grown and she had completely, as it were, a new set. The Lay Reader, bless him, did not get a new tooth and, in fact, subsequently had to sell a cow and get a false tooth. It's important to have a balance.)

I really do believe that in some of these teeth-fillings touches of God have come to people who are desperately poor and in no way would ever get treatment. This particular child was a tremendous witness, in that she was a member of the church and that because of her previous pain and knocking on doors, was very well known in the village and she went about showing people her new teeth and praise was given to God.

The same point is made by Dr Maxwell:

In 1976 there was an evangelistic campaign in Temuco, Chile, conducted by the Puerto Rican evangelist Yiye Avile, who had a powerful ministry, fasting and praying for many days before a campaign, with a big prayer back-up while the campaign was on. He was once 'Mr Puerto Rico' and a professional baseball player until he had rheumatoid arthritis. He was healed of this by Jesus and before long he was starting his own ministry. When people came up to testify to healing he would turn to the crowd and say, 'Who did this?' The reply came back, 'Jesus Christ.' He preached salvation first then prayed for the sick who came forward by their hundred. During his mission at Temuco I was examining patients in the stadium who claimed healing and wanted to testify. Outstanding in my memory were two girls aged between 12 and 14 years, in shabby clothes and shoes several sizes too big, etc. who were praising Jesus because they had experienced a tooth being filled. They looked too poor to have been able to afford a dentist but sure enough they each had a filling.

These incidents resulted in people becoming Christians. To quote Dr Maxwell again:

A nurse on the ward where I was working at the time – a paediatric ward of the government hospital, Temuco – told me how the carpenter repairing her father's house had become a Christian together with the rest of the family when one of their children came home from a meeting in the stadium with several teeth filled. Knowing she couldn't have gone to a dentist they acknowledged this to be the Lord working.

Why Fillings?

Well, why should the Holy Spirit have filled teeth miraculously? Three reasons present themselves:

1. God did this out of compassion for suffering, as he did in the gospels. That at any rate is clear. But the replacing of the carious teeth with whole ones would have achieved the same result.

2. As a witness to his power. There are two scenarios. In the first a child given brand-new teeth says to acquaintances or strangers, 'Look at my beautiful teeth – God's done a miracle.' To which the obvious answer is, 'Yes, those certainly are beautiful teeth. You've got a good Mum to give you such a sensible diet, and make you take such care of your teeth – I wish everyone's Mum was as thoughtful, keep it up.' (The kid was crazy talking about a miracle, but she's sure lucky with her parents.)

In the second scenario the child with miraculously filled teeth says, 'Look at my teeth – God's done a miracle.' 'Hey, look at these fillings. That's really something.' (What's going on? There's not a dentist doing fillings for fifty miles, and judging by that kid's rags she hasn't got the fare to the next bus-stop. We better look into this.) In other words the evidential value of fillings in such circumstances is the greater. And that it achieves such results is clear from the accounts already quoted from Chile.

That explanation might be the complete one, if it were not for Francis McNutt's American cases where dental care was available, so there must be a further reason. What can it be?

3. There is a view of miracles which sees them as natural biological phenomena, but where God has punched the 'fast run' button. And this must surely be true in most cases. In the woman whose chronic varicose ulcer was healed (Case Record 1.1, p. 10) presumably the vessels grew in, the fibroblasts multiplied and all the normal stages of wound healing occurred as they would naturally, but at miraculous speed. This in response to his divine will, without any human intervention.

However on occasion in his earthly life Jesus healed by use of means. Obviously there was no need for him to do so, for more often he achieved the same result by merely saying the word. But on at least three occasions our Lord used saliva (Mark 7:33; 8:23; John 9:6). Surely this was to make the point that medicinal substances have his approval. But of course it might be that this refers only to naturally occurring substances as used in wort-craft, and simples. There are always those who look doubtfully at anything made by human artifice, and who think it vaguely unspiritual that the Church should be efficient or use up-to-date techniques. They would be happier if I were to write with a quill and not a word-processor. But there are biblical precedents. Adam was told to subdue the earth (Gen. 1:28), which must, literally, have involved manipulating it. Later, in the wilderness journey when the time came to make the tabernacle, the Lord chose Bezalel son of Uri, and 'filled him with divine spirit, making him skilful and ingenious, expert in every craft and a master of design, whether in gold, silver, or copper, or cutting stones to be set, or carving wood' (Exod. 31:3–5 NEB).

I tentatively suggest that now, by filling teeth, God signals his approval, sets his seal of blessing on the use of technology. Man's healing skills and techniques are acceptable. In this specific case it is dental surgery (and when I spend most of a morning in a chair in the Newcastle teaching Dental Hospital I am glad about that), but obviously the implications are far wider, and not only for us in medicine.

An Unattractive God?

There is a more profound problem in these stories. We have seen that John Pridmore who published the incident from Chile, and stuck by it as an accurate record, could write after eight years consideration, 'A god who gives hungry people teeth rather than food is . . . pretty unattractive.' That is not the cry of disbelief, it is the agonising question with which God's people have wrestled in every age. In Chapter 1 we

184

noted Paul's questioning, and Barth's comments. It is very apposite to our present theme: why does God allow suffering in the first place? At a symposium on the hospice movement I heard one of its best known directors, Robert Twycross, admit to the temptation to go home and vent his anger on his family – anger at the unfairness of terminal disease striking down, for example, a woman still breast-feeding her baby. He told us that, as a Christian, he has learnt to direct his anger towards God, who is able and willing to absorb it. And who shares that anger. If we look at the story, recounted in all the synoptic gospels, of the leprosy patient who came to Jesus saying, 'Lord, if you want to, you can cure me', it is only Mark who refers to our Lord's emotional response (1:41). The Authorised Version uses the word translated 'compassion'. But there is an alternative reading which instead of speaking of Jesus' compassion speaks of his anger. The New English Bible picks this up: 'In warm indignation Jesus stretched out his hand'. When Jesus reached Lazarus' grave he wept (John 11:35). Tears surely not only of sorrow but of anger that his creation has been so spoilt by Satan.

Standing farther back we remind ourselves that that usurper is still the prince of this world. Those who are in rebellion against God, claiming the right to rule their own lives, cannot at the same time expect to share in the blessings of the kingdom. If God is kept at a distance he is kept at a distance. There is a war on, the purpose of which is to bring the peace and health of the kingdom to all, for it was planned for all; but even God cannot give the package to people if they will not take it. Meanwhile, inevitably, people on both sides are getting hurt. It is exactly the same problem as we looked at in Chapter 8. We want the earth and all its inhabitants to enjoy the good things God is longing to bestow; we want this *now*. But that is impossible before we get to the situation in which he can bestow them.

As a crude analogy, the picture is that of a besieging king who says to the starving sick garrison of the rebel town, 'Open your gates, I'll freely pardon you and pour in food and everything else you need, but I can't get these things to you while you shut me out.' Meanwhile, despite that, he catapults over the wall a few supplies. That is, of course, an inadequate picture, but the mystery of suffering is not solved in a paragraph.

One thing is sure. God suffers with us. He makes it clear to Moses that he grieves over the sufferings of his people in slavery in Egypt. What is even more amazing is to discover that he grieves for the sufferings – even those he has to impose on them himself – of Israel's enemies. In the prophets we read God's lament over Moab:

> 'The strings of my heart are plucked like a harp for Moab' (Isa. 16:11 JBP), and again: 'Therefore I wail over Moab, for all Moab I cry out, I moan for the men of Kir Hareseth. I weep for you . . . O vines. . . The destroyer fallen on your ripened fruit and grapes . . . I have stopped the flow of wine from the presses. . . In Moab I will put an end to those who make offerings on the high places. . .' declares the Lord. 'So my heart laments for Moab like a flute; it laments like a flute for the men of Kir Hareseth . . . for I have broken Moab'. (Jer. 48:31–8 NIV)

We are in it together.

1. F. McNutt, *Healing* (Notre Dame, Ave Maria Press 1974), pp. 327–31.
2. John Pridmore, 'Miracles; the Mystery and the Meaning', *Crusade* (October 1976).

10

Where have we got to?

For everyone who will take up his offer God's plan is perfect health. Wholeness at every level: physical, mental, spiritual. And each to a degree far beyond our imaginings.

For instance, on the spiritual plane we are to stand in God's presence not merely with our blameworthy past debited to Christ and therefore written off, but with a blank virgin-white record – not just blameless but faultless (Jude 24). As we are to be fellow-heirs with Christ (Rom. 8:17) can it be doubted that on the mental and physical level the perfection will be equally complete? Now all that is true, and marvellous, but its fulfilment is not on planet Earth in the present age.

There are those who talk and dream about 'sinless perfection' now, but with little supporting evidence. Surrounded as we are by the unbelieving world, bombarded by the media, is it possible to be uncontaminated? Ask yourself: when you hear of what some sadist has done to a small child do you not find yourself imagining with some gusto what punishment you would inflict on the culprit, echoing perhaps words from *The Mikado*, 'something lingering, with boiling oil in it'? You do not? Good for you! We would be no safer from contamination even if, eschewing the world, we were to enter a monastery and (in Thomas Merton's lovely phrase) 'be locked into our new freedom'.[1] All biography confirms that, even there, there would be no escape from the attentions of the evil one.

It is the same for complete physical health. The trees whose leaves are for the healing of the nations (Rev. 22:2) grow only in heaven. Before arriving there the Christian's body is at risk from bacteria and trauma. Even if it is claimed that we

187

will be protected from them we surely cannot expect a
personal radiation-shield, an individual lead-filter in our
lungs; or to go through life in our own bubble of pollution-
free atmosphere.

Is Longevity an Entitlement?

It is frequently stated that God's intention is that no Christian
should have a premature death. History denies this, and it is
a claim which could only be made of a truly democratic
country in peacetime.

What about the martyrs whose blood is the seed of the
Church? From Stephen in Jerusalem to the Baganda boys,
some not in their teens, who sang hymns as they were hacked
to pieces in that numinous spot outside Kampala, the young
have had their lives cut short for Christ. But we do not need
to go back a century; and, let us face it, it may not just be
in the past. In the late 1960s a student conference in Burundi
developed, unplanned, the theme of the glories of heaven –
into which many of the conference members were to be
bloodily ushered within the month. Should the Church have
gone without its seed? In 1962 I occasionally had patients in
a small hospital on Nakasero Hill, not dreaming that that
tranquil spot would soon become Idi Amin's torture centre
and killing ground: not least for some committed Christians
with whom we had fellowship. Was Archbishop Luwum out
of God's will when he was martyred at the age of fifty-five
one February night in 1977? It is also a point to think over
that for twenty years before these persecutions the Church in
Burundi and Uganda enjoyed God's blessings to an unusual
extent during the 'Ruanda Revival', and many of those
martyred were *balokole* – Christians who had entered into a
deeper spiritual experience.

What about war? Is there any evidence that Christian
aircrews, or come to think of it Christians under saturation
bombing, have a better statistical chance of survival than
their non-Christian friends? Have they, and our covenanting

forebears, cut down on the hills of Galloway, been out of God's will?

It is no use replying that martyrdom and war are unusual, the onslaughts of the devil. Of course they are, but I thought we had agreed that sickness came into the world through his activity.

Let us not forget pioneer evangelism. How many of the mid-nineteenth century missionaries in West Africa survived twelve months? Has all this been a mistake?

And what of ageing? Changes due to natural ageing processes and those due to disease can be very similar. When I am consulted by a patient with menopausal problems I often find it hard to draw a line between what is 'natural' – requiring only reassurance – and what it would be ridiculous to put up with, and for which I prescribe hormone replacement therapy. When does the nausea of pregnancy cease to be normal? When are aching joints merely due to age? I do not believe that we can always draw a clean line between health and disease. Because our children have had their childhood ailments they are protected by antibodies from infections which decimate unprotected communities. Was this a mistake? The sickle-cell deformation of red-blood corpuscles, which worries me in a coloured maternity patient in the UK, proves a defence against malaria in tropical Africa. I have not noticed that the writers who proclaim constant health for all believers define in what circumstances, or to what ethnic or cultural groups, this applies.

The Prosperity Gospel?

If we are entitled to what we consider the best physically, why not also the best in every other aspect of life? To look at one facet, everywhere in the first world but particularly in the American church scene many maintain that Christians can claim to be always not only healthy but prosperous. Surely they cannot have thought of the world-wide implications of that statement. It would not have sounded convincing to my fellow-servicemen, many of them Christians, who (less fortunate than I was) did not get away from Singapore in 1941. One man existed on berries in the Sumatran jungle until betrayed to the Japanese; another had more than sixty attacks of dysentery while working on the death railway in Siam. Even in the 1980s it would sound bizarre to multitudes of fine Christians in underdeveloped countries, who have to walk long distances to bring back polluted water from the river; whose greatest hope is to have a well in the village and for whom the barest facilities of civilisation – say, piped water or water-borne sanitation or electric light – remain beyond reach. But if an American Christian may expect God to provide a Cadillac, why should his brother in Ethiopia do without one? To Paul I suspect that the idea of guaranteed prosperity would have been strange, for he wrote to the Christians in Phillipi:

> I know what it is to be brought low, and I know what it is to have plenty. I have been very thoroughly initiated into the human lot with all its ups and downs – fullness and hunger, plenty and want. I have strength for anything through him who gives me power. (Phil. 4:12–13 NEB)

And his fellow Christians' experience was no different:

> Nothing therefore can come between us and the love of Christ, even if we are troubled or worried, or being persecuted, or lacking food or clothes, or being threatened or even attacked. As scripture promised: *For your sake we are being massacred daily, and reckoned as sheep for the slaughter* (Ps. 44:22). These are the trials through which we triumph, by the power of him who loved us. (Rom. 8:35–7 JB)

I suspect these claims to longevity and prosperity arise through the same tunnel-vision which I criticised in my introduction: a sole concentration on one activity of the Holy Spirit (the Bible), at the expense of neglecting his other activities, which we would notice if we were to obey our Lord's injunction and lift up our eyes and look on the fields (John 4:35).

190

St Paul's Health

Constant physical health was clearly not the experience of the New Testament Church: not of Timothy who was prescribed 'a little wine, for your stomach's sake' (1 Tim. 5:23) or, as we have already noted, Trophimus, whom Paul had to leave unwell at Miletus (2 Tim. 4:20) or of Epaphroditus (Phil. 2:30).

There is no doubt that God wants our health now – but what if spiritual and physical well-being cannot both be achieved simultaneously? How do we define health in those circumstances?

That this is a genuine problem is made crystal clear in Paul's own experience (2 Cor. 12:7–9). F. F. Bruce's paraphrase[2] of Paul's testimony reads:

in case the surpassing wonder of the revelations (given to me) makes anyone form an estimate of me beyond the testimony of his eyes and ears. Well then, to keep me from being unduly proud, I was given a bodily ailment, a sharp rankling pain, a messenger of Satan to keep me under and prevent me from becoming too proud. I prayed to the Lord about this three times and begged Him to take it away. But he said to me: 'My grace is all you need: my power is most fully displayed when my people are weak.' This taught me a lesson and now I will rather boast in the things that expose my weakness, and that right gladly, so that Christ's power may take up its abode in me. This is why I rejoice in my infirmities, in the injuries I suffer, in my privations, my persecutions and distresses; I rejoice in them for Christ's sake, for it is when I am weak that I am truly strong.

That passage is so important for the debate on healing that we had better unpack it. Paul's own words are 'a thorn in the flesh'. Those who are unhappy at the thought of the prince of apostles being other than perfectly healthy suggest that this thorn was spiritual, or that it refers to human adversaries[3] or satanic attacks or sexual temptation, or even to a wife. For lengthy discussions on this, Tasker's[4] and Alford's[5] commentaries should be consulted. From the latter it seems clear to me that this refers to a physical ailment. If not, then Paul's words 'in the flesh' are surprisingly ill-chosen for such an able wordsmith. I am prepared to accept as definitive Kittel's classical *Theological Dictionary*:[6]

> In 2 Cor. 12:7 Paul is speaking about bodily affliction . . . that is obviously painful. The idea is not that of a stake to which the apostle is impaled, nor of a barb of depression, e.g. at his failure to win the Jews to Christ, or in reaction from ecstasy. Physical ill-treatment or a physical disability seems to be in view. . .

God had the choice: he could work towards Paul's spiritual or his physical health. As the former was more important he was willing to refuse Paul's prayer for physical healing in order to fulfil his deepest desire:

> I count everything sheer loss, because all is far outweighed by the gain of knowing Christ Jesus my Lord, for whose sake I did in fact lose everything. I count it so much garbage, for the sake of gaining Christ and finding myself incorporate in him. . . All I can say is that I forget the past and I strain ahead for what is still to come; I am racing for the finish, for the prize to which God calls us upwards to receive in Christ Jesus. (Phil. 3:8–9 NEB; 13–14 JB)

At the end of the day however the commentators' arguments about whether this was a physical or psychological thorn prove to be unimportant, for if the latter it was still 'dis-ease'. And therefore whether 'dis-ease' or disease Paul was allowed by God to keep it so that his real health on the spiritual plane might be advanced.

'If it be Thy Will'

When we reach God's presence there will be no question of either/or: we will be completely healthy. In Chapter 8 (p. 167)

I mentioned my local pastor and his fatal cerebral tumour. During his illness, every morning in her devotions one of our fellowship was given some word from the Lord which she felt was appropriate. She would write it on a piece of paper and drop it through the manse letter-box on her way to work. On the day he came out of hospital the word she received was: 'I will heal him in my nearer presence.' Shattered, she did not have the courage to deliver that note, and months later dredged it out of her handbag to show me.

The question each of us asks when we fall ill is: will he heal me here? Wanting my best, here and now, as he does, is physical healing that best? The short answer is: we cannot know but we are entitled, we are invited, to ask him.

So, following our Lord in Gethsemane (Mark 14:36), we have to pray, 'Father, I would like to be rid of this burden, and you can take it away, but I don't know what you know to be best for me. If it is your will please heal me physically.' That phrase 'If it be thy will' has been the source of great controversy. It has been called 'the faith-denying clause'. Yet not to employ it suggests that we indeed know what is best for ourselves.

We have no mandate to say what is the best for us. So we come to our Father and say, 'If it be thy will', knowing as we leave the situation in God's hands that we will have his best. While we are not granted to walk in a disease-proof capsule, 'we have been allowed to enter the sphere of God's grace, where we now stand' (Rom. 5:3 NEB). This point is well taken by the West Indian patient in our next record. The gynaecologist involved allowed me a sight of the complete case notes.

CASE RECORD 10.1

In late July 1976 a black lady aged thirty-six was referred to the gynaecological unit of a hospital in London, with a grossly swollen abdomen. A few days later at operation her abdomen was found to contain two litres of blood-stained fluid, there was a partly solid tumour of the left ovary the size of a fetal head, stuck to all surrounding tissues, main vessels, and throughout the pelvis. Only part of the mass of the right ovary was removed with great difficulty, but the uterus was too embedded in growth for hysterectomy to be possible. Obviously malignant tissue had to be left behind, stuck on to the rectum. A cytotoxic drug, poisonous to cancer cells, was instilled into the abdominal cavity before the operation was concluded. (This was classified as IIb, Advanced Granulosa Cell Tumour of moderate mitotic activity, but with obvious metastases.)

Before the operation the patient, a Christian who was and is an enthusiastic leader in her local pentecostalist church, had made the gynaecologist promise to tell her the findings post-operatively. They had prayed together. This promise was honoured, whereupon the patient sat up in bed, and shouted down the Nightingale ward, 'Listen everyone, I've got cancer which could not all be removed. Either I'm going to go to Glory or Jesus is going to heal me. Hallelujah!' Her local church were specifically praying for her healing, and believing.

She was treated with radiation, but this tumour is poorly sensitive to such treatment. However at follow-up there was no evidence of tumour. At the present writing she is approaching her ten-year tumour-free survival.

Reading through her notes, there is one letter which is as significant as it is unusual. It is addressed to the patient by the gynaecologist, and reads in part: 'I wonder if you would mind coming back to out-patients next Monday about four o'clock to do a great good turn for me? The doctor who anaesthetised you for your operation has now got a similar problem. She remembers anaesthetising you and I think it would cheer her up tremendously to have a talk with you.'

The gynaecologist writes to me: 'The joy in her (which made her radiant throughout) was of her expectancy of seeing *"in what way"* her Lord was going to act in this situation for His glory: whether to take her to Himself or heal her.'

It will be noted that this patient had a higher criterion than 'my health/survival': it was 'his glory' that mattered.

A Time Tag on our Prayers?

A refusal to employ the rider, 'If it be thy will', involves not only results but timing. It implies a belief of entitlement to physical health – *now*. Those who will not go so far avoid that last word, saying that we can confidently expect healing but not necessarily now. For all practical purposes that attitude completely invalidates the claim, because until the healing comes (in a month, six months, ten years) the sufferer remains ill. Moreover it is essentially an escape clause to cover up the absence of the promised cure.

In no other field do we put a time-tag on our prayers. There are some things we can ask in absolute confidence that they are in God's will – the spiritual welfare of our nearest and dearest, for example – but even in those matters we do not feel entitled to say '*now*, Lord'.

The Holy Spirit's Activities: always the same?

Part of the problem is that the New Testament healings occurred either at once, or almost at once. It is often said that, unless we are dealing with some spurious 'gift', surely the same should be happening nowadays. Should it? Why? Is there any evidence – even in the Old Testament – that at any moment in time God froze his pattern of working, never to vary it thereafter? The foundation event for the OT people of God was the Exodus. That idea, blossoming in the hand of God as he comes to deal with us, is illustrated by the splendid transliteration, which I cannot trace, of Luke 9.31, where, on the mount of transfiguration, Moses and Elijah talked with our Lord, 'of the Exodus which he should accomplish at Jerusalem'. The details of the second exodus are different from those of the first; but by them both God's people have been brought out of bondage.

On the day of Pentecost God the Holy Spirit poured out on each and every disciple the gift of power and the gift of tongues. But no gift of healing. But by the time that Paul was writing his first letter to the Corinthian Christians, only twenty-five years later, two things had happened: while each Christian had gifts of the Spirit these were far more differentiated; and no one had them all. So Paul asks the rhetorical questions: 'Are all apostles? all prophets? all teachers? Do all work miracles? Have all gifts of healing? Do all speak in tongues. . . Can all interpret?' (1 Cor. 12:29–30 NEB). We have noted many activities of the Holy Spirit which in different ages have not been constantly the same. And surely to God (literally) this is what we would expect a God who is a living God, and not a fossilised one, to do. That is what we do for our own children, reacting in love appropriately to their stage of development, their ever altering circumstances, and the swiftly changing world in which they live. Would we expect God to do less?

We can demonstrate this same versatility of God's in the ecclesiastical scene, where we know only too well the difficulty of any attempt to re-establish the pattern of the early Church. What pattern? Do we mean that of the early episcopacy? Or the congregational presbyterian set-up? Or the assembly of the brethren? Or, earlier still, the commune? Our attempts prove to be a waste of effort. Maturity surely requires the ability to relax and thank God for what he is showing us in our day. Of course *my* fellowship is right on the nail, and within it *my* personal theology is the most on target: alas for such smugness! As we progress it becomes abundantly clear that God is showing different fellowships different things.

My point is that all the deep heart-searchings, and all the great debates designed to prove/disprove that present happenings – such as healing miracles – are/are not the genuine copper-bottomed New Testament gifts of the Spirit, are unnecessary. The enterprise is futile, being misconceived. Surely it would be very worrying today if we were *back in the apostolic Church*, when we are not living in the Roman Empire of the first century. It would imply that God the Holy Spirit had lost interest, that he was out of touch. If his gifts in c. AD 54 were a maturing of those in c. AD 29, is it not logical to expect a further maturing (not a withdrawal nor an impoverishment but an enrichment) by the late 1980s?

Gifts to the Body

In the field of miraculous healing it seems that today, while the Holy Spirit still gives certain Christians an individual gift of healing, he is also giving it in a general way to the Church. Tom Smail, a leader of the charismatic movement, tells that in the church in Belfast of which he was minister, when someone asked for prayer for healing he would reject any request that one particular member of the eldership should do this. Instead he would ask two elders – the next two in line, as it were – to lay hands on, and pray with the sick person. Thus it was made clear that healing is the work of the Holy Spirit through the Church. But it is not altogether a new idea. When 800 years ago an ill woman from St Albans was told in a vision to go to Christina of Markyate for healing, the latter refused to pray for her until in the presence of a priest: 'the others could join with her in praying for the mercy of God on the matter', so that the grace of recovery should not be attributed to her.[7]

We have already noted (p. 114) that in one of his miracles our Lord did a double healing (Mark 7:33–6). My next case-history demonstrates this; but more important for our discussion it shows the ministry of healing being exercised by the whole body – in this case the people who happened to be sitting alongside. It was brought to my attention by a general practitioner, a lifelong friend of the patient. The record is abridged from details supplied by the patient himself, now an architect; and his family doctor has sent me the 1971 x-ray report: 'Fairly well marked osteoarthritic changes affecting the knee joint. Two fixation screws are seen in the shaft of the tibia.' He has also confirmed that his patient needed analgesics regularly until the mid-1970s but adds, 'He has had no further prescriptions since that date, nor has he consulted us for anything below the waist at all since then.'

CASE RECORD 10.2

In 1950 Mr J.S., then aged twenty-seven, was knocked off his motor-cycle and sustained injuries to his right leg: compound fracture of the tibia, fracture of the fibula, dislocated hip joint. Attempts at reduction of the dislocation having failed he was put on traction with pins through both hips and right leg just below the knee. After ten weeks in hospital he was discharged with hip-to-toe plaster. The tibia and fibula failed to unite, screws and bone grafts were employed. He was first allowed to walk without the aid of crutches or stick nine and a half months after the accident, but the plaster was not removed for a further two months. It was another year before knee mobility and partial ankle mobility were regained, leaving him with a 2 cm shortening of the right leg: a shoe with 2 cm raise was prescribed. At a medical examination in connection with his claim for compensation he was warned that within ten years he would have 30 per cent disablement through arthritis of the damaged joints.

By the early 1970s his GP was having to prescribe pain-killers for the ankle and knee pain, and especially for the deep-seated hip pain. After ten minutes walking he had to rest for five minutes before continuing. An x-ray confirmed arthritis. He was becoming more and more morose and disillusioned even in his Christian experience.

In 1976 on a silver-wedding visit to his brother's church in Canada: 'on entering its doors we could almost physically feel the Presence and Love of the Lord Jesus. At the end of the first Sunday evening service, an invitation was given for those with needs to go to the front for prayer and laying on of hands. I went forward, was prayed with and immediately received healing from all my arthritis and have not since then taken any medication for that complaint. After returning to England my daughter complained that she could not keep pace with me when we were out walking and asked me to walk more slowly.' He was also emotionally and spiritually renewed. He was able to spend twelve hours a day up and down ladders, re-roofing his house.

Although his arthritis had completely gone he continued to wear his built-up shoes, and the muscles of his right leg were wasted. Nearly three years later, in 1978, at a conference those wishing prayer for healing were asked to stand, then sit so that those on each side could pray for them for whatever was needed. In seconds his right leg grew the 2 cm to equal exactly the left one. Within two or three months the muscles also became fully restored. 'I still have my built-up shoe and sometimes use it to demonstrate what God has done for me. I never cease to be thrilled by the sight of it projecting 2 cm beyond the sole of my left shoe. Wearing normal shoes, as I now do as a matter of course, my heels are both perfectly level one with the other. When Jesus was ministering with His disciples, He caused the lame to walk. He still does! It happened to me!'

A Protocol for Divine Healing?

When I first met cases of miraculous healing, and became interested in what God is doing in this field, I decided that one day I would sit down with all the case histories I could collect and identify the patterns. I would aim to elucidate God's criteria, find out the methods Christians should use and get some systematic guide-lines worked out. That is the standard method of medical investigation. However from the Case Records presented one thing is clear – there is no pattern.

In some instances the patient prays, in others friends pray. Some people have such faith that they pray once only: for others 'soaking prayer' is used: a team praying in relays over a protracted period. Usually those who pray are present, but sometimes they are miles away.

The elders of the church may be sent for, following the instructions of the apostle James (5:14–15), and the patient is anointed with oil. But there is no obvious definition of 'elder': in our Nepalese Case Record (4.1, p. 74) those involved were three expatriate missionaries and an indigenous carpenter.

At large meetings where many are healed the missioner lays hands on the patient and prays; at others Christians around him are bidden to pray. The patient is not always touched physically.

In some cases the person ministering has a recognised gift of healing; in others this is so far from the case that he (or she) takes a great deal of persuading that this involvement is God's will, clearly made known. He or she (the Holy Spirit shows no sex-discrimination) may be ordained – episcopally or otherwise, or a layperson, mature or teenager. Denomination affiliation is of no importance nor is there evidence that 'shepherding' or 'covering' makes any difference.

Sometimes prayer is specific: for the raising of the dead or for healing without residual disability; on other occasions it is that God will be glorified whether by life or by death.

God's healing can be surprising: dental fillings rather than new teeth; the preservation of physical well-being in a case of haemorrhage but without stopping the bleeding before nature does so.

In some cases healing is complete and instantaneous, in others it occurs in stages; it can be spontaneous – without warning – while daily prayer is being offered for the condition.

There are cases in which God gives a word of knowledge where the cause is undetected: Kathryn Kuhlman stood and announced what specific healings God was doing in the auditorium (in other words she exercised her gift of knowledge) and only then did the already-healed come forward.

Perhaps all this explains why the Holy Spirit inspired Paul to write about gifts of healing in the plural.

Not only is there no pattern of method, there is no pattern for knowing who will be healed by God, or how it will happen.

CASE RECORD 10.3

As a preamble to this case let me mention a Christian lady who comes to Sunderland for treatment, and is gifted by the Spirit. On her I have performed four major abdominal procedures, each resulting in the formation of more adhesions than the last. (Adhesions are the gumming together of the abdominal contents, and are associated with chronic pain which can be very wearing.) She has been much prayed over, for a number of years. Together with the wife of one of the elders of our fellowship I have visited her in her home; we have anointed her with oil and prayed over her. Physically she is no better.

This case refers to another of my patients, also a Christian, on whom likewise I have performed four abdominal operations, finding gross adhesions. (I hasten to add that this is unusual in my practice.) After her last operation when she was aged thirty-nine, I made the note (for the benefit of my successor) that I strongly advised against further abdominal surgery, which could not involve less than pelvic clearance, with the emotionally traumatic implication of surgical menopause. Shortly afterwards she came back to see me in despair as she was now having to take so many analgesics that she felt incapable of carrying on with her work as a nurse. I did not know till months later, but she told a friend that she was going to ask my opinion about prayer for her problem. Before she could do so I suggested it to her. The difficulty was that I knew she was a member of an active 'sound' evangelical church which did not appear to be enthusiastic about the present manifestation of the charismata. So I put it to her that as I was just going away on holiday she had a fortnight to think it over; on my return she should phone me, and if desired I would arrange with a group of friends to pray for her healing. On the day of my return she called to say that she had plucked up her courage and spoken to her own minister. He and the elders had prayed for her. She had had no pain at all since. Many months later, at the present writing, that is still the case. She has needed no analgesics at all.

We cannot pin down miraculous healing. This is because we are dealing not with a thing, but with a Person. God the Holy Spirit, the hurricane who gusts where he wills, who will not be pinned down. Because he loves us he individualises his care for us. And that care sometimes surprises us and astonishes the honest medical observer.

A Final Proof

The following case was reported in 1984 by the girl's parents to Dr Anne Townsend, who, recently returned from medical missionary work, was editing the Christian magazine, *Family*. Dr Townsend passed it on to me. With the parents' permission I have been able to obtain confirmation of the medical details from the ear, nose and throat specialist concerned.

CASE RECORD 10.4

At a school medical in September 1982 the suspicion that this nine-year-old girl (whom we will call Rebecca) had some hearing loss was confirmed. Audiograms and tympanograms showed a hearing loss of 70 decibels in her right ear, and 40 in her left. 'The consultant confirmed that she was nerve deaf in both ears and there was no cure, no operation, nothing he could do. We were shattered . . . God soon reassured us that it was good we now knew she was deaf . . . so that she would be able to hear with the help of hearing aids.' It was likely that she had been deaf for about five years since measles or mumps, both of which she had had when aged four.

Rebecca 'didn't want to wear hearing aids for the rest of her life so she started to pray that God would restore her hearing'. On 3 December 1982 Rebecca got her first hearing aid. Despite initial vomiting she adjusted and persevered with it, and was soon wearing two.

Her mother writes: 'A friend and I had started to meet for prayer and I felt that I should pray for Rebecca's healing, but I was afraid in case it wasn't what God wanted to do. However Rebecca continued to pray and I encouraged her, although she did know that God might have a purpose in her being deaf and she must accept that if it was His answer. We all prayed, and many friends prayed, we know. I kept feeling God was telling me to pray specifically for healing. Passages kept coming out at me as I read. "If you have faith like children", "If one among you is ill, lay hands", "Ask and you shall receive", "Your faith has made you whole." Eventually I thought that when a child if I had wanted, for example, a biscuit I wouldn't have sat around wondering whether or not my mother would give it to me – I would just have asked. As God was my father I was going to ask Him. On the day of His arrest Jesus asked God, "If it be your will remove this cup of suffering from me." I was no longer afraid to ask but would accept God's reply; Rebecca mattered as much to Him as she did to me, and she was in His care. He has a plan for her life.'

In February Rebecca had her adenoids removed and myringotomy performed. 'We were well warned that this would not alter her hearing but was preventative. The next morning she said she had turned down one of her aids one mark. The consultant said there was no reason for her doing this as her nerve deafness was much greater than any middle-ear deafness. We took this as a sign that God did want to heal Rebecca so we all prayed in faith, and in complete trust, and with conviction that God was leading us to pray.'

On 8 March 1983 Rebecca had to attend the audiologist to obtain a new hearing aid as one of hers was damaged at school. Next night, at 9.30 she came running down from bed to say, 'Mummy, I can hear!' 'I couldn't take it in. I tested her and she heard everything we said, even whispers.

I knew what the disciples had felt like when they prayed for Peter's return from prison and he arrived at the door (Acts 12:12–17). The three of us knelt and gave God thanks. Then we phoned the consultant who said, "I don't believe you. It is not possible. All right, if some miracle has happened I am delighted. Have audiograms done." ' Next day, 10 March, Rebecca's audiogram and tympano-gram were normal. Her hearing was A1 normal. 'The audiologist came out with moist eyes and said, "I can give no explanation for this. Rebecca's audiograms are normal. I have never seen anything like it in my life." The consultant sat and ruled out all the possible medical explanations. After repeat audiograms he said, "Forget she ever was deaf." ' The mother concludes, 'God's timing was remark-able, the fact that Rebecca's aid was damaged the day before her hearing returned emphasised that her return of hearing was instantaneous. The audiologist knew she was deaf the day before.'

In view of the importance of this case I will quote further from the medical report of the consultant ENT surgeon.

He confirms the audiogram figures, adding, 'There was no conductive element present in the audiogram and this audiogram was done with masking and was very accurate.' She had also a large pad of adenoids in her naso-pharynx, a left indrawn tympanic membrane and possibly fluid in her right middle ear. 'Her problem therefore was twofold. One was an untreatable bilateral sensorineural deafness and the other was middle ear catarrh with Eustachian obstruction especially on the right side, with enlarged adenoids adding to her problem.'

She was coping fairly well with hearing aids but was still having a problem with mouth breathing and snoring. On 2 February 1983 bilateral myringotomy was carried out. Fluid was sucked from the right ear. Left middle ear clear. Adenoids removed.

She was seen two weeks later and was very well indeed but

naturally still very deaf from her sensorineural deafness and requiring still to wear her hearing aids. Approximately three weeks later she was rather distressed one morning to find one of her hearing aids not working at all well. This proved a great problem for her with her hearing loss and she was seen by the audiometrician. Repair of the hearing aid was carried out, much to the relief of the patient who could now hear normally with the help of both aids.

Two days following this, for some inexplicable reason her hearing returned completely to normal and on 10.3.83 an audiogram did show her hearing in both ears to be totally and completely normal. I was completely unable to explain this phenomenon but naturally, like her parents, I was absolutely delighted. She was reviewed on 15.5.83 and once again an audiogram was completely normal.

I can think of no rational explanation as to why her hearing returned to normal, there being a severe bilateral sensorineural loss. (my italics)

Conclusions

We have reached a position where certain assertions appear valid.

1. Intellectual honesty demands that (after discounting cases with dubious diagnoses, those where psychosomatic considerations are important, and others where the cure might be attributable to adjuvant medical therapy or where spontaneous remission might be the explanation) there remain some cures for which medicine has no explanation.

2. That in these cases the constant association of prayer to God cannot be discounted. Nor can it be set aside as merely a psychological 'boost', for some of these healings cannot have a psychosomatic explanation.

3. These kind of healings, which occurred widely during the ministry of Jesus Christ and, after the resurrection, during the work of the Church, did not cease at the end of the apostolic age nor at any other point in time, but have occurred

with varying frequency throughout the history of the Church, and are still being seen.

4. That although Christ purchased health on the cross, as well as redemption and adoption as God's children, the benefits of none of these can be fully entered into during our earthly life.

5. Healing is not an automatic response to an adequate quantity of faith, nor is it withheld if insufficient faith is generated. Nor does it require correct theological understanding. It is in the sovereign will of God.

6. The Christian is entitled to bring all problems, including health, in prayer to God, but is not entitled to lay down what particular answer he should give, or at what time. We can make bold and specific requests as long as we do so 'if it is thy will'.

7. Intellectual honesty requires us to acknowledge that our experience today (by any definition that is acceptable) is that only a small percentage of those for whom physical healing is sought from God obtain it. But in absolute terms the number appears to be fairly rapidly increasing as more churches become open to this work of God; and percentage-wise more are being healed as the Holy Spirit is being permitted to develop ministries within local fellowships.

8. A belief in the occurrence of cases of miraculous healing today is intellectually acceptable. The conclusion seems inescapable, in the light of the evidence presented in this work, that we have a living God, intimately interested in our affairs, prepared to intervene in a specific practical way in response in prayer. This being the case it is logical to pray about our health, and that of our patients and friends.

1. T. Merton, *The Seven Storey Mountain* (New York, Harcourt Brace Jovanovich 1948; and London, Sheldon Press 1975), London edn, p. 372.
2. F. F. Bruce, *An Expanded Paraphrase of the Epistles of Paul: in chronological order with a connecting narrative.* Exeter, Paternoster 1965.
3. C. Urquhart, *Receive your Healing* (London, Hodder & Stoughton 1986), pp. 239–41.

Where have we got to?

4. R. V. G. Tasker, *The Second Epistle of Paul to the Corinthians*. London, Tyndale Press 1963.
5. H. Alford, *The Greek Testament*, rev. E. F. Harrison. Chicago, Moody Press 1968.
6. G. Delling, in C. Kittel and G. Friedrich (eds), *Theological Dictionary of the New Testament*, abr. and tr. G. W. Bromiley (Exeter, Paternoster; and Grand Rapids, W. B. Eerdmans 1985), p. 1047.
7. C. H. Talbot (ed.), *The Life of Christina of Markyate: a twelfth-century recluse* (Oxford University Press 1959), pp. 46–7.

Index

abdominal pain 42
abortion 8, 42, 55, 56
abscess 52
adhesions (intra-abdominal) 201
Adomnán 141
Aelred of Rievaulx 112
Aethiwald of Melrose 73
Aidan of Lindisfarne 77, 111
ageing 43, 189
Alford, Dean 18, 146, 192
Allbut, Sir C. 53
amnesty, divine 81
anaemia 45, 61
Ananias of Damascus 133
Anglo-Saxons 4, 73
Anne, Queen of Scotland 85
anointing with oil 69, 73, 99, 170, 200,
    201
antibodies 189
apostolic credentials 132
Apostolic Fathers 134ff
appendicitis 100
arbitrariness; see unfairness
Askew, E. 5
asthma 30
atonement and healing 159–164, 206
Augustine of Canterbury 73
Augustine of Hippo 55, 69, 79, 135–7
authority of Christians 86, 157
auto-immune diseases 2
Avile, Y. 182

Bairstow, E. 98
baptism in the Spirit 95, 99, 100, 201
Barth, K. 19, 185
Baxter, R. 89
Baxter, S. 141

Bede, Ven. 21, 27, 47, 73, 75, 77, 88,
    141
benign disease 28
Bennett, D. 101, 102, 103
Bezalel 184
Bible 5, 52, 147
    translations quoted:
        AV Authorised Version (King
            James) passim
        GNB Good News Bible 44
        JB Jerusalem Bible 45, 125, 190,
            192
        JBP New Testament in Modern
            English; and Four Prophets (tr.
            J. B. Phillips) 43, 186
        NEB New English Bible passim
        NIV New International Version
            passim
        RSV Revised Standard Version 7,
            145
biblical criticism 111
    interpretation 110
blackwater fever 51
bladder carcinoma 45
blindness 31, 58
Boddy, Mrs 100
body of Christ 133, 197
Bonser, W. 21
Booth, W. 48
Bothelm 75
breast carcinoma 30
Bridge, D. 11, 72, 147
British Medical Association 54
Bruce, A. B. 159
Bruce, F. F. 191
Brown, C. 110, 129
Brown, P. 79, 81

Browne, S. G. 65
Budgen, V. 135, 146
Burma 51, 116, 161
Burrswood 57

Cadbury, H. 142
Calvin, J. 55
Campbell, Duncan 150
Campbell, Isobella and Mary 94–8
Campbell, Macleod 94
cancer; see neoplasm
canon of Scripture 146
carcinogen 25
cardio-vascular incident 15, 104
Caring Professions Concern 66
Carothers, M. 42
case-history approach 3, 4, 7, 20, 137
CASE HISTORIES
  abscess 52
  adhesions 126
  backache 164
  blindness (partial/permanent) 20
  breast tumour 158
  carcinoma of bladder 45
  coagulation defect 60
  fibrosing alveolitis 25
  fractured pelvis 76
  hernia (strangulated) 35
  hip pain 102
  meningitis 20
  myocardial infarction with
    ventricular aneurysm 104
  nerve deafness 202
  ovarian carcinoma 193
  raising the dead 139
  return from the dead 138
  ruptured spleen 74
  stress incontinence 164
  traumatic leg shortening 198
  varicose ulceration 10
  viral hepatitis 116
  visual disturbance 31
Castlesteuart, Lord 85
Celtic Church 73
certainty as to outcome 20, 101, 140
charismata 2, 3, 5, 71, 88, 94, 98,
  130–152, 196
charismatic renewal 8, 59, 70, 104
chemotherapy 80
chest pain 74
Chile 139, 176–84

China Inland Mission 51
Christian Medical Fellowship 3, 171
Christina of Markyate 197
Chrysostom 135
Church's ministry of healing 50ff
Church of England 50, 55, 78, 101
Church of Scotland 56, 81
Church Missionary Society 49, 61
Clark, K. 139, 178, 181
Clemoes, P. 78
clergy-doctor co-operation 56–7
clinical caution 29
Clyde, Firth of 93–8
coagulation defect 60ff
Coggan, R. 60
coincidence 14, 27
Cole, W. H. 25
Colgrave, B. 75
Columba 77, 141
compassion (divine) 18, 183
confessional 42
Confession of Faith (Scots) 144
confirmation (episcopal) 98
congenital disease 43
Copernicus 64
coronary artery disease 30
counselling 53
Cranmer 146
Cunningham, W. 143
Curé d'Ars 13
Cuthbert of Lindisfarne 27, 73, 80, 88,
  93
Cyrus, King 6

Damien, Father 159
death, definition 139
  welcomed 47
demons (see spirit world)
dental fillings 175–84, 200
desert Fathers 72, 112
diabetes 29, 104
diagnosis, incorrect 7, 27
  retrospective 28–9
dispensational views 7, 63, 112, 130–52
Divine Healing Mission 53
Dodd, C. H. 18
Donald, I. 60
Duke, J. A. 69
Dunn, J. 115, 163
Durham 73, 146

Eareckson, Joni 169

eczema 102
Eddius Stephanus 75, 77
Edinburgh Medical Missionary Society 48, 50
Edmunds, V. 3, 5
Edwards, J. 146
Elijah 75, 87, 138
Elisha 75, 79, 87
emotions 30
encephalitis 40
endocrine factors 25, 30
Esau 18
Eucharist 105
Eusibius of Caesarea 135
evangelicals 57
Evangelical Sisters of Mary 75
Everson, T. C. 25
Exeter, Bishop of 55
Exodus 87, 195
exorcism 113ff, 134

faith mandating healing 5, 155–7, 165–73, 206
Fancourt, Miss 29, 96
Fawcett, A. 149
fever 25, 69
fibrinogen 61
fibrosis of lung 25
Finucane, R. 78
food multiplied 13, 14, 38, 121
food-poisoning 51
forgiveness of sin 30, 43, 81, 187
Foster, R. 78
Fox, G. 112, 142
Fractures 75–6
Free Church of Scotland 88
Frodsham, S. 98
Frost, E. 134, 135
fundamentalism 7, 53
Fursa 141

Galileo 64
Gindiri revival 35, 72, 151
globe of fire 72
God's honour at stake 75
guidance (divine) 36
Guild of Health 52, 58
Guild of St Raphael 57
gut lesions 14, 171

haemorrhage 74, 167, 200
haemorrhoids 99

Hagin, K. 155
handkerchiefs 79, 129
Harper, M. 101
healers 33, 55
HEALING
  as by-product of ministry 102, 103, 113
  definition 42ff
  double 114, 197
  gifts of 197, 200
  integral to other gifts 102, 108, 130
  partial 46
  perfected 19
  services 26, 46, 99
heaven 43
Heavenfield, battle of 77–8
Henry VIII 79
Henson, H. H., Bp 53, 110
hepatitis 116
hermeneutical questions 11–12
hernia 35, 37
Hexham 75, 77, 81
Hezekiah, King 79
Hickson, J. 53
hip disease 29, 96
historians' attitudes 12, 21
Hoare, F. H. 70
Hocken, P. 148
homes of healing 57
hospital chaplains 57
Howie, J. 81, 86
Hubbard, R. 159, 160
Hume, D. 11, 39
hysterectomy 23
hysteria 29, 54

'If it be thy will' 192ff, 206
illness, freedom from 1, 155ff
immune mechanisms 30
infections 25, 189
Institute of Religion and Medicine 57
intracranial growth 28, 167–8, 193
invocation of saints 78
Iona 77
Ireneus 134
Irving, E. 94, 97

James 5:14–15; 51, 74, 99, 200
Jansenists 40
Jerome 69
Jesus' miracles 29, 107, 108, 113–24, 184

use of means 114
worked through Holy Spirit 112–22
John of Beverley 80
John the apostle 44, 122–5, 133
Johnson, D. 3
Josiah, King 78
Justin Martyr 134

Kee, H. C. 12
Kelsey, M. 136
Kendrick, G. 160
Kennedy, J. 88
Ker, D. 97
Kerr, Munro 4
kingdom of God 45, 113–22
King's Evil (scrofula); see tuberculosis (glands)
Kirkton, J. 82, 85
Kirkudbright 83
Kittel 192
knowledge, gift of 72, 88, 200
    word of 126, 147, 193
Knox, J. 78, 82–3
Kuhlman, K. 112, 149, 200

Ladd, G. E. 148
Lambeth conferences 53, 59
Laurentin, R. 38, 39
laying on of hands 10–11, 33, 56, 76, 116
Lazarus 44
leprosy 48, 69, 74, 107, 119
Lewis, C. S. 4, 15, 107
Lightfoot, Bp 78
Lindisfarne 73, 75, 81
Ling, Mrs 138, 141
Livingstone, D. 49
Livingstone, J. 85, 87
Lloyd-Jones, D. M. 44, 63, 64
longevity 188
Lourdes 38, 103–6
Luwum, Abp 188
Lysenko 64

Maddocks M. 53, 72
Maddox C. 51
Mark 112–16
Markus, R. 135
Martin of Tours 67–72, 79, 93, 137
martyrs 79, 188–9
Matthew 117–19, 159–60
McCrie, T. 97

McCulloch, W. 149
Macdonald family 29, 94–8
McLewrath, P. 87
McNutt, F. 112, 164, 175, 183
McPhail, H. 88
Maxwell, W. 178, 180, 182
measles 25, 202
mediaeval miracles stories 16, 78
Melinsky, M. A. H. 8
meningitis 20, 167
menopause 23, 189, 201
menorrhagia 23, 69, 119
Mennonites 132
mental history 128
Merton, T. 187
Messiah 111–12
Methodists(ism) 32, 98, 142
Mews, S. 59
Meyvaert, P. 21
migraine 30, 32
mind 30, 42–3
MIRACLES
    alternative explanations: 23ff, 44
    antithesis to scholarship 2, 21
    disbelief in 11, 17, 21, 39, 70, 82, 110
    nature speeded up 16
    other than healing 38
    proof of 2, 63
    worked by Holy Spirit 112
miraculous healing, definition 1, 12, 15, 17, 28, 67
    purpose 44, 113–125
missionary experience 49, 50–2, 113, 189
Moab 186
monastic tradition 47
Montupil, A. 139–40
Moody, D. L. 142
Müller, G. 13
myocardial infarction 104

Naaman 18, 107
natural history of disease 25, 35
nausea of pregnancy 189
neoplasm 2, 24–5, 28, 30, 45, 167, 171
Nepal 74
neurological conditions 28–9, 32
New Testament canon 146
Nicodemus 6, 143
Nigeria 10, 35, 72, 151
Ninian 69

Northumbrian saints 27, 72ff.

oil, volume increased 71
ophthalmic conditions 20, 31, 58, 102
ordination 50, 105, 200
Origen 135
organic disease 1, 30
orthodoxy, medical 48, 50, 126
  theological 103, 143
orthopaedic conditions 27–8, 75, 102,
  164, 166, 197
Oswald, King 77ff, 93
ovarian lesions 12, 80, 193
Overseas Missionary Fellowship 65,
  138

Packer, J. 12
paediatric conditions 25, 40, 43, 189
Pakistan 60
paralysis 29, 69
Paré, A. 15
Paris, François de 39, 40
Paul (Saul) 18, 43, 133, 191
Peddie, C. 54
pelvis fracture 76
Pentecost 101, 108, 111, 142, 145, 196
pentecostals(ism) 51, 100–1
peptic ulcer 30
perfection 145
Peter 112
Pharisees 6, 152
Phypers, D. 11
physiological explanation 23, 31
Picts 141
pilgrimage 78
placenta praevia 60
pneumonia 20
pneumothorax 26
poisoning 69, 115
Polycarp 134
Pool of Bethesda 17
Possidius 136
power, spiritual 71
prayer chain 28
prayer-cloths; see handkerchiefs
prayer groups (meetings) 40, 104
Presbyterians(ism) 8, 82, 88
Pridmore, J. 176, 181, 184
Prior, D. 146
Proculus 134
prognosis, fatal 26
prophecy 7, 83, 145, 147–9, 151

prosperity gospel 189
protocol for divine healing? 106–7,
  195–7, 199, 200
psychosomatic conditions 29, 59, 108

Quakers (Society of Friends) 132, 142

radiation 25
raising the dead 69, 84, 129, 134,
  137–41, 200
Ramsey, I. 2, 8
Ranger, T. 50
Ravensbruck concentration camp 71
regression of tumours 25
remission (spontaneous) of disease 24,
  31, 41, 168
revivals of religion 146, 149–52, 188
Roger of Hovedon 16
Roman Catholics(ism) 39, 42, 51, 64,
  104
Roman Empire 6, 16, 68, 80, 88, 141,
  197
Rose, J. 3
Row, J. 82
Royal College of Obstetricians and
  Gynaecologists 60
Rudder, P. de 103

Sabbath-keeping 6, 123
sacraments 53, 54, 56, 57
Salvation Army 48, 99
sanctification 100
sarcoma 24
Satan (the Devil) 8, 52, 54, 75, 156, 164,
  185, 189
scepticism (healthy) 23
Schlink, B. 75, 77
scientific approach 2, 4
Scorer, C. G. 3, 5
scotoma 15, 20
Scottish reformers 81–8, 137, 141
Scrimger(eour), J. 85–7
Seekers 132
sensitivity to treatment 25
Severus, Emperor 134
sex discrimination 200
Short, Rendle 3, 173
shrines; see relics
sickle-cell trait 189
Sigel, A. 179
sin defeated 161ff
Slim, Field-Marshall Sir W. 161

Smail, T. 197
Smithers, D. W. 25
snakebite 69, 115
Society of St Vincent de Paul 106
South American Missionary Society
139, 178
spirit world 51, 54–5, 72, 115, 118, 138,
152, 171
splenic rupture 74
Sri Lanka 143
Stancliffe, C. 68, 70
starvation 17, 184
Stockdale, W. 164
Stewart, J. S. 42
Strachan, G. 108
stress diseases 30, 35
stroke (cerebro-vascular accident) 104
Suenens, Cardinal 108
suffering 156–7, 184–6
Sulpicius Severus 69, 70
Sunderland 11, 100, 142
Swinburne, R. 39
symptoms disregarded 172–3

Talbot, R. 138
Tasker, R. V. G. 192
temptation in the wilderness 117
Ten Boom, Corrie and Betsie 71
Teresa (Mother) of Calcutta 159
Tertullian 134–5
testimony to healing 89–90
Thailand 138, 140–1
Thérèse of Lisieux 47, 94
third world 177, 184, 189–90
Thirty-Nine Articles 144
'thorn in the flesh' 191–2
throat tumour 89
tongues, singing in 87
speaking in 38, 94, 97, 100, 115,
142–3, 145, 196
toothache 175–84
transfusion 62, 74, 116

Trench, Abp 44
Trowell, H. 57–8
Trevenna, John and Eileen 142
tuberculosis, of glands 85
of lungs 47, 94, 156, 173
Twycross, R. 185

Uganda 1, 8, 51, 67, 132, 188
ulcers, varicose 10, 12, 183
Urquhart, C. 155–6, 169
unfairness of God 17–18, 184–6

V-Day 162
Vitricius, Bp 80

waiting for answer to prayer 71, 76, 138,
140
Waldensians 48
Walls, A. F. 50
war 189–90
Ward, B. 11–12
Warfield, B. B. 103, 107, 132–7
Waterhouse-Friderichsen syndrome 20
Watson, D. 171
Welsh (Welch) J. 82–5, 141
Wesley, J. 48, 111, 149
Whitefield, G. 149
wholeness 42, 44, 64, 187
Wigglesworth, S. 54, 98–101
Wilfrid of Hexham 75, 77
William of Malmesbury 12
Williams, C. P. 50
Williams, David and Bridget 151
Williams, J. R. 148
Wimber, J. 151, 171
Wishart, J. 83
Woolston, T. 17
World Council of Churches 56
Wyclif 64
wound infection 103

Young, J. 82